I Come from Crazy

Tia Angelo

Cover illustration by LuAnn Arena

BALBOA.
PRESS
A DIVISION OF HAY HOUSE

Balboa Press books may be ordered through booksellers or by contacting:

Balboa Press
A Division of Hay House
1663 Liberty Drive
Bloomington, IN 47403
www.balboapress.com
1 (877) 407-4847

Because of the dynamic nature of the Internet, any web addresses or links contained in this book may have changed since publication and may no longer be valid. The views expressed in this work are solely those of the author and do not necessarily reflect the views of the publisher, and the publisher hereby disclaims any responsibility for them.

The author of this book does not dispense medical advice or prescribe the use of any technique as a form of treatment for physical, emotional, or medical problems without the advice of a physician, either directly or indirectly. The intent of the author is only to offer information of a general nature to help you in your quest for emotional and spiritual well-being. In the event you use any of the information in this book for yourself, which is your constitutional right, the author and the publisher assume no responsibility for your actions.

Any people depicted in stock imagery provided by Thinkstock are models, and such images are being used for illustrative purposes only. Certain stock imagery © Thinkstock.

Print information available on the last page.

ISBN: 978-1-5043-7478-1 (sc)
ISBN: 978-1-5043-7480-4 (hc)
ISBN: 978-1-5043-7479-8 (e)

Library of Congress Control Number: 2017902189

Balboa Press rev. date: 02/20/2017

For my two beautiful children with love

Contents

Part Three

Acknowledgments

From the deepest place in my heart, I want to express my gratitude and love to everyone who has loved and supported me in my life and in the birth of this book

To my big-hearted, husband for quieting my fears and wiping away my tears through this process. Thank you for your endless love and support and for believing in me. I could not have done this without you.

To my children my greatest gifts in life. Thank you for your unconditional love and your bravery while walking through this crazy life together.

To my one and only sister, I could not imagine this journey with out you. From day one, we remain forever bonded. I love you more than words can express.

I do not know where I would be without my extended family. I thank my amazing aunts and cousins for always accepting me. It takes a village, and if it were not for you, I do not know how I would have made it.

To all of my friends who have loved me through this life and on this writing journey, you know who you are. I am eternally grateful for your love and friendship.

Writing can be lonely, had it not been for my fur baby Bella always in my lap or by my feet as I wrote.

Alisia Levitt my amazing writing coach! There is no way I could have completed this book with out you. Thank you for the many sessions we had together. We cried and we laughed and you made me believe this book could be a reality.

Gabrielle Bernstein, my friend, teacher and mentor thank you for helping me face my fears and thank you for reminding me that the light I see in you is a reflection of my own light. Deepest gratitude to you and your teachings.

Introduction

This is the true story of my life—the life of a girl who grew up in a crazy, dysfunctional family, as many of us have.

This is a story about a resilient girl raised by an alcoholic and drug-dependent mother, who also had a loving dad who tried his best.

This is a story about a girl who moved often, going to seven schools in twelve years, learning how to be the new girl, and hiding her secrets about her home life while triumphantly climbing her way out of the dysfunction of her crazy family.

Many people told me that I should write a book about my life because my story is a story that needs to be told.

Friends and therapists throughout the years have told me that my story is unique, so I should share it with the world. And I have not really shared my story with many people until this point. Even my closest friends never knew what my life truly was—until now.

I have always loved writing and have kept a journal since the sixth grade. On the school bus on the first day of yet another new school, I was feeling scared and frustrated, so I started writing my feelings in my spiral notebook.

This is a story about a girl who never had a voice and saw many things that no child should. No matter what occurred in my home on any given day or night, I went to school or out to play with my friends and never said a word to anyone about my life. Maybe I thought it was normal.

When I got into therapy after my dad's death, I started sharing my life with my very first therapist, Laura, I told her stories about my life like someone would tell you about a routine day. She looked me in the eye and told me that my story was incredible and far from the norm.

I stayed in therapy most of my adult life, and years later, my then therapist pleaded with me to write a book. "It will be a best-seller and maybe even a movie," she said. So I began to write a few pages about the early years of my life, starting with my very first address in Brooklyn, New York. I began each chapter with the next address I moved to, and that's how it started to take shape. Although I had to change some of the addresses to get the book published it mostly remains the same.

I decided to title the book *I Come from Crazy*. The thought occurred to me after having dinner with one of my dear friends Joy, and her family. At one point during our meal, her son and daughter got into an argument, and her son turned to his sister and said, "Let's stop this. Tia is going to think we're crazy."

I turned to him and said, "Don't worry about it, I come from crazy, so there's nothing you can say that would surprise me."

After drafting several pages, I decided to show them to one of my dear life long friends. When we were down at the Jersey Shore for a girlfriend weekend. I wanted to show her first because I trusted her; we had been friends for over forty years, and we were both avid readers. I waited patiently while she took the pages back to her room to read. I felt vulnerable but excited.

She brought them back to me a while later and said, "This sounds really good, but you need to embellish more," and that's when I decided I couldn't write a book. Doubt and fear took hold of me, and my dream of writing a memoir was snuffed out by those few words. I just didn't have faith in myself as a writer. My ego had taken that little bit of constructive criticism and had a field day with me.

The other thing she said was, "Wow, I never knew any of this about you." It occurred to me that my life, though very dysfunctional to other people, was just *my* life. I thought everyone went through it: the craziness, the drugs, the moving from one place to another, the alcohol, the mental illness. And no one knew any of it because I kept it all inside.

I put the idea of a book out of my head, but I still had a burning desire to write my memoir because I wanted to get my story out there to inspire others. I wanted others to know that if I could make it in this crazy life, so could they. If I could help change the life of even one person and give him or her hope, then it would be worth it.

The shift came one night while attending a book signing for my spiritual teacher, Gabrielle Bernstein. Her fourth book, *Miracles Now*, had been released, and she was promoting it. During her talk, Gabby said, much to my surprise, that she had a tenth-grade reading level and that it was amazing she was on her fourth book. At the end of her talk, she referred to someone in the audience who helped her write her book—her book coach. She said this woman had made her words "pretty and shiny and bright" on the page. It was a light-bulb moment for me. I thought, *Someone helped her write her books. What was I thinking to try and do this on my own?*

Several months later, I was invited to a workshop by a local therapist who had just written a book. After her talk and before her book signing, she referred to someone in the audience who helped her write her book, and she mentioned a women by the name of M.J sitting in the back row.

I made a mental note to get M.J' s phone number. So I emailed the therapist the next day and called M. J. as soon as I could. I felt the universe was saying, "It's your time." I sat back down at my computer and started writing again.

It's been a very cathartic, spiritual, and at times painful journey for me. Being vulnerable is not easy. I cried, laughed out loud and prayed a lot!

My hope for this book is that it will inspire, uplift, and give hope to you. I want you to know that no matter where you come from or who raised you, you're in charge of your own destiny. Your happiness is in your own hands. As they say in the metaphysical text *A Course in Miracles*, "Only love is real." Find the love in every situation, and let it start with you. Love yourself for who you are, where you came from, and where you are going. Happiness is a choice we make. Let it be your mission in life. It took me a long time to believe that everything could be okay and that I deserve to be happy. It's something I work on every day, shifting from fear to love, sometimes minute by minute.

My hope is that *I Come from Crazy* will be a starting point for you in truly loving yourself and every aspect of who you are, where you came from, and the miracles that await you. And I hope you have a few laughs along the way.

With massive love from my heart to yours,

Tia

Part One

For he will give his **Angels** charge concerning you.
To guard you in all your ways…
Psalm 91:11

Pastina with Butter and Milk

Ingredients:
    1 cup pastina
    2 or three teaspoons of butter
    ½ cup milk
    Salt and pepper to taste

Directions:
    Bring 2 cups of salted water to a rolling boil. Add in pastina. Cook approximately 10 minutes, or until the tiny star shaped pasta is soft. Pour into a bowl and add butter and milk.

Mrs. A's Mayonnaise Cake

Ingredients:
    2 cups flour (sifted twice)
    2 teaspoons baking powder (leveled)
    1 cup sugar
    1/2 cup cocoa powder (sifted)
    1 cup mayonnaise
    1 cup cold water
    1 teaspoon vanilla

Directions:
    Blend all ingredients together and pour into greased 9-inch cake pan. Bake at 350 degrees for 25 minutes.

Chapter 1

A Girl Born in Brooklyn, Brooklyn, New York

I'd be lying if I said I felt normal. Never, ever have I felt that way.

When I was a very young child, something *always* felt off. Watching my mother on her hands and knees, scrubbing the floors in the hallway of our apartment building in Brooklyn, bothered me. It was a big, wide, mosaic-tiled hallway. I used to sit on the steps as my mother told me to wait patiently until she was finished. Years later, I asked why she scrubbed the floors, and she replied, "To save money on the rent." For some reason, something about watching her scrub the floors frightened me.

I have vivid memories of that little apartment and the happy time I spent there from infancy to age three with my father, and mother. Don't ask me how I have such clear memories, but I can clearly describe our second-floor apartment as cozy, with a decent-sized kitchen, living room, and two bedrooms. The apartment had very modern 1960s furnishings. I remember the hissing of the steam from the old cast-iron radiators and the sound of traffic horns from the street below. It was a comfortable place to live, and I felt safe.

The heart of our home was its small, bright kitchen. The walls were papered in beige with a pattern of brown diamonds and stars. We had a fridge and a washing machine next to the kitchen sink. There was a little stove in the corner and a small wooden table that family and friends gathered around.

We had a big Italian family that stood by each other no matter what. My mom was one of six girls, and she was the second to the oldest. So I had my aunts around me all the time. My parents had lost their first baby, a girl, at birth five years earlier. I was a gift and felt very much loved.

My parents met on a blind date in 1956 when my mother was eighteen and my father was twenty-one. They quietly eloped. After finding out that my mom was pregnant. My grandmother eventually had them marry in a church, once she found out. It wasn't unusual to marry at a young age back then. (It's hard to come up with the exact details here. My aunts can't always remember much, so I'm going by my own memory and my sister's memory from the stories we heard over the years.)

My parents settled into a quaint apartment in downtown Brooklyn, where they had both grown up, close to their family and friends. Unfortunately, their plans for a family and a sweet life together came crashing down when the baby was born prematurely and lived for only nine hours. They named her Lucia. My parents were, of course, devastated.

My dad went home and took apart the nursery before my mom got out of the hospital. My mom was quite sick after that. It took her a very long time to recover and five more years to get pregnant again. Sunny, summer day in 1962, I was born to two very happy parents. They finally had a sweet baby girl to fill their days and brighten their lives.

My mother was a stay-at-home mom at that time and kept our home neat as a pin. She was a clean freak, washing the kitchen floors in our home on her hands and knees. You could perform surgery in any corner of the house. As a toddler with a pretty face and big cheeks, I took baths in the kitchen sink. Every Easter, my dad brought home soft, fluffy baby chicks for me. Before they eventually went to the farm, my mom gave them baths in the same sink.

My early days in Brooklyn were filled with fun trips to the park, bus rides to visit my grandmother, and playing on the fire escape, looking up and down the street as I waited for my father, the great love of my life, to get home for dinner.

Mom would always have a meal prepared for dinner, and the kitchen always smelled of onions and garlic. She was great at making homemade sauce. Every Sunday was macaroni day. She'd make meatballs and macaroni, and dinner was early at two. On some Sundays, we went to downtown Brooklyn to my grandmother's house.. She made the same exact meal of meatballs and macaroni, and it was so *good!*

My all-time favorite food to eat was pastina. It would become the comfort food of my life. To this day, there is nothing like a hot bowl of this tiny, star-shaped pasta with milk, butter, and salt. My only other way to eat pastina was with Sunday sauce. I eventually would serve it to my own babies, and to this day, when my daughter does not feel well or has a rough day, I offer up a bowl of pastina.

The only thing that comes close to pastina would be peas and macaroni, as my family referred to it. Our version was a very light tomato-based soup with small shell pasta and a can of peas. Heaven. I love memories of food and family, especially meals shared with my father.

Dad worked hard. He had two jobs: He worked as a laborer for the city by day and cab driver by night. When I was little, I thought he was Superman. He was tall, dark, and handsome with a great mustached smile that made his brown eyes sparkle. Dad smelled like Old Spice and tobacco and teasingly called himself Joe Cool after the snoopy character.

He actually claimed to be Superman, and I really believed him. That went on for a while until the day he cut himself. I was amazed that he was bleeding because Superman did not bleed.

I remember the smell as Dad smoked Larks cigarettes with the charcoal filter. He also liked a little Scotch and water or a Rusty Nail every now and again. He was a happy and very friendly person.

Everyone knew that he was very generous in every sense of the word. He was always willing to lend a helping hand and went out of his way to help the family. That was the kind of person he was, no questions asked. He was known to help friends and family get a job if they needed the work. He tried to help everyone have a better life because he knew how hard it could be.

Dad had been very poor growing up. His parents were Italian immigrants. My grandfather worked at a shipyard, painting ships, and he was killed when he fell off some scaffolding. My father was only two when it happened. By the time he was five, he was shining shoes on the corner.

Dad told me stories of being hungry. One day, when he was really hungry, he stuck his fingers inside of all the candy and nut machines in his neighborhood because he didn't have a penny to buy something. He finally found one treasure inside: a pistachio nut. Dad said it tasted like steak to him.

My father dropped out of high school to join the army. After his tour of duty, he got a job as a laborer working for the city of New York, fixing potholes and shoveling snow when necessary. He rose up the ranks, and by the time he died, he was second in command in his department. He made sure all the roads were paved and pothole-free. To this day, when I smell hot asphalt, I think of him.

I had a great relationship with my dad. He was truly one of my best friends. I was "Daddy's little girl" for sure. He made me feel pretty, special, protected, and much loved. He provided everything that a daughter should feel from her father. To say that he made a huge impact on my life would be an understatement. He was the first man I ever loved, and he taught me how to love and be loved and cherished. From what I understand he made my sister feel the same way, we can both argue over who was his favorite to this day.

When people ask me about my mother, I say it's hard to describe her because her emotions were a roller coaster. She wasn't grounded and reliable like my father was. On the outside, she was seemingly a happy person. Most people that met her thought she was a relatively normal, nice housewife and mother.

My mother was a very pretty woman. She kept her hair short and frosted for most of her life. She had pretty, dark-brown eyes and gorgeous skin, and she was religious about putting her makeup on first thing in the morning before she went about her day. Her go-to routine included a signature cat eye black liner, Jean Naté splash, and Jean Naté powder applied with a big puff she kept in the bathroom. Sometimes when I go to CVS, even after all these years, I open a bottle of Jean Naté and take a whiff to catch her scent.

When I was older, I went onto the fire escape, where I could look out at the street and the front of the building. We lived on a pretty, tree-lined street. On nice days, I used to sit up on the fire escape, holding my mother's keys. I liked to be the key holder. I usually ended up accidentally dropping them down onto the sidewalk. Random passersby would hear the jingle of the metal as the keys hit the concrete and scoop them up for me. I would always ask my mother for the keys and promise not to drop them, but I always did. In some ways, wanting to hold my mother's keys is symbolic of the role I would take on later in childhood—being forced to grow up quickly and to parent my mother at times.

My mom's best friend, Natale, and her husband, Sonny, lived across the street with their son, Michael, Natale was her best friend from childhood; they had grown up in the projects together. She was very pretty with red hair, a sparkle in her eyes, and a quick smile. I loved her, and I still love her today.

Michael and I were born four months apart in 1962. He was such a cutie! We had a baby crush on each other, and I was sure he would be my husband. We played in the playpen while our moms gossiped and drank coffee. Michael and I went for many a carriage ride, and when we got a little older, we held hands any chance we could. We were best friends. It's funny that I would eventually marry another man named Michael.

My mom's five sisters were always over at the apartment, and since I was only the second grandchild born, I was spoiled by all of them. My aunts' names from oldest to youngest are Viola, Lucia, Peggy, Connie, and Ruby. My grandmother had the three younger girls with her second husband, Mike, and the first three girls were already grown by the time she had the second three. The three older girls, including my mom, were separated from their mother after she divorced their father. My grandmother became ill at that time, and the girls went into foster care. They were babies and had already been through rough years, as their dad was an alcoholic and very abusive to my grandmother.

There were nights that my mom had her sisters, Natale, and another girlfriend or two over to play cards. They would sit at the kitchen table, laughing and chattering, with a big jar of buttons that they used for chips. Buttons of all colors and sizes rested in piles on the table. Those "girl" nights were fun.

Out of all my mother's sisters, Aunt Ruby was my favorite because she was only nine years older than me; we kind of grew up together. She obviously was much younger than my mom, and she would sleep over at their apartment on occasion. I remember hearing the story about Ruby wanting to know why my parents had green water. Actually, they had a green bathtub. She'd sit in the tub and sing the song "Johnny Angel" over and over again. Years later, during darker times, Aunt Ruby was always there for me, lifting me up and making me laugh.

When I was two, Ruby was eleven. She was very pretty and dressed like a hippie with peasant shirts and flowing dresses, bell-bottom jeans, and leather belts. She truly had her own style. Ruby was bubbly and funny, kind but tough, and extremely smart.

When my mom visited my grandmother, Ruby had to drag me all over Brooklyn; she was kind of stuck with me. Times were different then, and nobody worried about abductions or anything of the sort.

I remember her taking me to confession with her one day. She told me I could come into the booth with her if I was very quiet. She said that when she had finished confession, and if I had behaved as promised, she would take me to Parisi's candy store on the corner of my grandmother's street for penny candy.

Parisi's was one of my favorite places on earth. We would get big, red wax lips, candy necklaces, and flying saucers. (They are kind of like two communion hosts put together with tiny candies inside.) The perfect end to our candy spree was, of course, bubble gum. We spent a nickel apiece—not a bad deal. However, there was always the part when Mrs. Parisi would pinch my cheek really hard and say, "*Coma si bella, coma si bella.*" Translated into English, that means, "You are beautiful." Ugh. But the candy was worth the pinch.

My father's mom, Constance, lived in the same neighborhood in Brooklyn, so sometimes Ruby and I would stop there as well. On some Sundays, I would visit her with my dad. She lived with my Uncle Nate, who was not quite right. Constance was a short, plump, old-school Italian grandma. She wore housecoats and rolled her black stockings halfway down her legs. She was always very kind and sweet whenever we were together. I spent a

lot more time with my mom's family, so my memories of her are
few. She died when I was eighteen, so it's been over thirty-five
years since I've seen her. I wish I'd had more time with her and
gotten to ask her many questions I have about her life and Italy.
She spoke both Italian and Spanish because one of her best friends
was Puerto Rican.

I don't want to say that Uncle Nate was mentally challenged,
but coming from crazy means no one explains anything. When
they do, trust me, you can't believe a word they say because it is
misconstrued, too. The story of Nate goes something like this:
One day when Nate was a baby, he was playing on a fire escape
and fell off onto his head and was never right after that. I would
imagine that the fall damage his brain. I never knew exactly what
happened after that.

But Uncle Nate was a good, kind man. He ran errands for
everyone on his block. For a small fee, he'd pick up your groceries
or dry cleaning, walk your dog, and basically do whatever you
asked. He was quiet and humble, and in my heart I knew he was
harmless, but I was still a little leery of him.

So those first years in Brooklyn were really special, and I thought
it would always be that way, as any child would. I'm not sure
when my mother's addictions started. From what I understand,
they had already started then but had not reared their very ugly,
grotesque heads. Overall, I felt very much loved by my parents,
aunts, grandmothers, and family friends during my earliest years
in Brooklyn. I didn't begin to see the change in my mother and
her mood swings until later. Looking back, I see that life on Four
hundred Forty-Third Street was wonderful compared to the years
that followed.

My father decided it was time to move out of the city he had lived in his entire life and move us to Long Island. I think the move out of Brooklyn was simply for my parents to get out of the city and into the suburbs, where they would buy their first home. We moved into that lovely old home with pretty peaked windows that I can also remember very clearly. It was two stories, and I had my own room at the top of the stairs toward the back of the house. My parents' room was next door—a bright, sunny room at the front of the house. It had been heated with coal at one time, and there was coal in the basement and also edging the garden.

We had wonderful neighbors and seemed to be surrounded by family and friends. I remember everyone coming over to visit and spending one Christmas there. I got many toys and dolls, and I felt very happy and safe. I always was outside playing with the neighbors' children in our yard or theirs. Life was easy and fun. I was three years old.

After living there for a year or two, my mother missed her family because her sisters were all buying houses and moving to Staten Island. The Verrazano Bridge, also known as the Ginny Gang Plank, had been constructed. Being Italian I can say that phrase. This resulted in most of her family packing up and moving out of Brooklyn across the bridge to Staten Island.

That's when we moved to Our little house on Staten Island, and slowly, without warning, my life changed into a nightmare that continued for twenty-five years.

Chapter 2

My Little World, Staten Island, New York

In 1967, Staten Island was still mostly farms and woods. However, after the Verrazano Bridge was completed, it made it easier for people to move in, and little bedroom communities started to pepper the island.

Dad purchased our house for $14,500, and the property was his little slice of forty-by-one hundred heaven. In Staten Island, the first few years seemed blissful and fun. With lots of children in the neighborhood, I made many new friends. The Marino's lived across the street, and they had five girls and were expecting their sixth, who would also be a girl. I always wanted to be one of them because they had very nice parents and an incredibly cute Chihuahua named Gonzalez.

My parents had barbecues with my mom's family. My aunts would come with their husbands and my cousins, and we'd have wonderful summer days. Some of my fondest memories were swimming and playing in the pool with my dad and having make-believe shows with my friends in the backyard, under the weeping willow tree. I remember Easter egg hunts with real hard-boiled eggs that we colored together and Christmases filled with toys, food, and family. The first Christmas or two in our new little house were wonderful. We had a tree that spun around and flashed lights, and I got lots of dolls and toys.

One of my favorite things about Christmas throughout my childhood was Christmas Eve. We would all go to Grandma Lucia's house, wherever she was living, and have a gigantic fish dinner, referred to as the Feast of the Seven Fishes. My grandmother would serve steaming bowls of blue point crabs in a red sauce over linguini. She would make snails in a red sauce; we plucked them out of the shells with safety pins. There was also fried flounder and fried shrimp and baklava. We would start the meal with a cold seafood salad that consisted of calamari, scungilli, shrimp, and black olives with lemon and olive oil dressing. I learned to eat this way from a very young age, so I was never squeamish about eating anything. I could not wait for the day I could grow up and have Christmas Eve at my own home and cook that delicious feast.

When I was in kindergarten, I was a typical girly girl. I was happy to play with my dolls. I was also still Daddy's Little Girl. My admiration for him continued to grow, and I loved him with all my heart and looked up to him. He was my everything, and I knew I was his. I loved my large family, and believed I was safe within it. My aunts and grandmother were always around me, and at that time, my mom was still healthy. I was not yet afraid to be around her; other than having a short fuse at times, she was okay.

Most Friday nights, especially during Lent, we ordered pizza and spaghetti with mushrooms in a thick marinara sauce. This was one of my favorite meals of the week. Dad would go to the pizzeria in town to pick up the food, and Mom would set the table with a bright-blue and white plastic tablecloth and paper plates. It was nothing fancy, and there was no dish washing on that night. I would have a slice of pizza, but my favorite thing to do was to make a spaghetti sandwich. I would take a piece of the Italian bread that came with the meal, slice it in half, and pile on the spaghetti. If there was any ricotta on the table, I would top it with that, put the other piece of bread on top, and eat the most delicious spaghetti sandwich. I was a skinny little thing, so my parents loved to watch me eat.

I believe that my life was good then and that I was taken care of as a girl of five years old. I trusted that that world was a safe place.

But then things started falling apart.

It began with having to suddenly switch from public school to Catholic school just as the semester began. I had attended kindergarten in a local public school and started first grade there as well. For some reason, about a week or two into first grade, Mom and Dad decided I should go to Catholic school. So off to Mary of Faith School I went.

It was the start of many scary and unpredictable changes. I remember being very frightened the first day, and I cried while Sister Jude, the principal, walked me to my new classroom. My teacher, Sister Mary Alice, had her sidekick, "Old 36"—what she lovingly called the yardstick that she used for disciplining. I never got hit because I was too afraid to do anything wrong, but lots of others did. After watching several children have to bend over a desk and get whacked on the behind, I decided that was enough for me to keep quiet. This was also the start of being "the new girl."

Almost everyone in the class had gone through kindergarten together and had already been in this first grade class for two weeks. It was the beginning of many changes in schools and friends. I went to seven schools in twelve years and never left the city, let alone the state.

My sister, Andrea, was born in 1967, and I was so excited to have her in my life. I was the big sister, being five years older, and loved every minute of it. My mother had a C-section, which involved some complications, and she was never the same, it seemed to me. Apparently, the doctor nicked her bladder, and she had to go back into the hospital to fix the problem. It was her fourth time being opened up.

My mother was never good at resting after coming home from her surgeries, and she began to develop adhesions, which would be a problem for the rest of her life and ultimately led to her death. She was prescribed Darvon for pain for her recovery and for the back pain she was having. That is when things shifted for the worst.

I have heard from my family that my mother had issues with prescription drugs before that time, but it became evident in the house that year. There was some talk of Darvon and why she was taking so many. I was not sure what to make of this at six years old. And it only got more complicated. It's amazing that my mother's Darvon addiction, coupled with excessive alcohol, didn't kill her sooner.

My mom had a reverse reaction when she took Darvon. Instead of getting drowsy or sleepy, she got wired. She walked around with her eyes really wide and with lots of energy. When she drank while on Darvon, she got sloppy and slurred her speech. Even if you didn't know her, you would know she was stoned or drunk. She would fall asleep at the table or just about anywhere she was sitting up. Sometimes she would even go missing. Many times a kind stranger would bring her home or call our house and let us know where she was so we could pick her up. She would come home muddy or with blood-stained clothes because she had fallen. Somehow she always got home.

I remember hearing the saying "God looks out for drunks and babies." Maybe this was true for my mother, but he did not save her from her addictions. I can remember my grandmother, Lucia, coming over and spilling a bottle of Darvon on the table. The half-gray, half-clear pills were filled with colorful little balls, like nonpareil sprinkles. They littered the table, and my grandmother was screaming that these were "the root of the problem." She was right. My mother was addicted to Darvon for the next twenty-five years—with shoplifting, arrests, and insurance fraud included.

This addiction was also the root of what made me feel unloved by my mother. I always felt that she loved her pills and drinks more than me and my sister—or even my dad. There had to be a reason she was anesthetizing herself with alcohol and Darvon. If I had to guess, I would say that she was dealing with anxiety and depression. Whatever was underneath the surface had begun to affect our daily lives in a major way.

My relationship with my mom was okay. But she was always so sick and in and out of hospitals that it was hard to form a mother-daughter relationship. Many times I felt more like the mom. But when she was coherent, she was a good mom to me. She always made dinner and got Andrea and me ready for bed at night.

Yes, when she was not in the hospital and when she was stable, she could be a good mom, but those periods became rare. Most of the time my life with her was chaotic and unpredictable. You never knew when she would be drunk or stoned or have a seizure. One day she'd be good and the next several she would be a total mess. I was never at peace when I was alone with her.

I clearly remember the epileptic seizures she started having when I was in first grade. One morning, I was waiting by the front door for a ride to school from my next-door neighbor and his daughter. My mother was standing at the top of the stairs, and when I looked up to her to say good-bye, her eyes suddenly glazed over. She tumbled down the stairs in a heap, convulsing and foaming at the mouth. It was sheer terror for me; I thought for sure she was dying. It's horrible to witness anyone have a seizure, let alone being a six-year-old watching her mother in this state. After the convulsing stopped, I thought for sure she would never wake up, but she did.

And it went on like that.

I was very afraid to be alone with her because we never knew when she would have another seizure. I'm sure that's when my anxiety started kicking in. It got to the point where I could always tell when my mom was about to have a seizure. She would stop in her tracks, and her eyes would glaze over. Sometimes she would even shout out, "Oh my god, it's happening!" and then fall.

My heart would start to race, and I would start to shake. I always ran to her side to try to hold her down and keep her arms from flailing about. She would foam at the mouth, and I was always afraid she would swallow her tongue because I was told that could happen. I thought, *If that happens, she will die for sure.* Of course, that terrified me, which increased my anxiety. After the shaking stopped, it would take a few minutes for her to come to. It felt like hours, and I was always sure she was dead.

For a girl age six, the fear of her mommy being dead before her eyes is almost impossible to put into words. It is a mixture of anguish and heartbreak, hopelessness and terror. I would always sit beside her and *will her* to wake up. I prayed that she would open her eyes and come back to me.

Now, if I try to search for something positive to remember about my mom, I would say that she showed me how to be kind and loving. Despite her addictions, seizures, and mood swings, she was a very kind and friendly person. She loved her family and friends with all of her heart and with all she knew how. However, this was overshadowed by so many bad memories that if I tried to remember them all, the list would be too long and painful.

My parents and grandmother decided that the pretty, little house was bad luck and that we should move. This would be the beginning of many bad decisions and moves, and many, many schools.

Chapter 3

The Crazy House,
Brooklyn, New York

Although friends and neighbors affectionately referred to the house in Brooklyn as "The Crazy House," it was never really my home. I don't believe I even got mail there. However, I lived there a lot, so it's important to tell you about it. I spent most of my life crossing back and forth over the V.Z. Bridge from Staten Island to Brooklyn, and here's why.

All three of my youngest aunts, Peggy, Connie, and Ruby, lived in Brooklyn in the same house with my grandmother, Lucia. When my other aunts and grandmother first moved there, my aunt Connie lived on the first floor with her husband, Mark, and her two children, Mark and Mary. Peggy lived on the second floor with Uncle Andy and her son, Mark. (Yes, they both named their firstborn Mark! Aunt Connie did it for the obvious reason, and Peggy because it was Uncle Andy's father's name.) I stayed with all five of my aunts on and off. My two older aunts Viola and Lucia named after my grandmother lived a few blocks away.

I can remember being really young and staying over at my aunt Lucia's apartment in Brooklyn. My aunts Lucia and Viola always lived together to some degree. In this particular house in Brooklyn, Lucia rented the downstairs apartment with my Uncle Tim, and Viola rented upstairs with Uncle Fred, her husband. I can remember staying over there quite a bit. I was the second niece, and they loved having me around. They would babysit me every chance they could. But that was just now and then.

Over at the crazy house, my grandmother lived on the top floor with my aunt Ruby, who was a teenager at the time. Ruby and I were only nine years apart. She was my favorite, and over the years we became good friends. At that time, the house had an unfinished basement. Eventually, as Peggy's family grew and she needed more space, the basement got finished and became an apartment for my grandmother and Ruby. Peggy took over the two top floors, and Connie stayed on the first floor.

As time moved on, Connie divorced. Ruby eventually got married and then moved one more time; she took the basement apartment with her husband, Rick. Peggy moved to the first floor with her four boys, Mark, John, Gerard, and Donald. And Connie moved upstairs with Mary, Mark, and my grandmother. Phew.

I went back and forth from sleeping in the basement apartment with Grandma and Ruby. After my aunt Connie divorced, I slept on the first floor with her. I was always a little on edge because, first of all, I was afraid of her dog, Remmy—not for any good reason other than German shepherds scare me to this day. The other reason was because my aunt Connie would have to smoke her last cigarette of the night in bed with the light off. I would lie next to her on my side and watch her smoke. I remember the bright-red embers and the ashes that she flicked into a nearby ashtray and the way she would smoke her cigarette down to the filter. I stayed up and watched this routine every night because I wanted to make sure she put it out so she didn't burn down the house. I didn't want to die in my sleep.

Once in a while, I slept on the top floor with Aunt Peggy and Uncle Andy. I loved my uncle, and truth be told, he was and always will be my favorite uncle. Aunt Connie and Uncle Mark got divorced when I was very young, and I never really got to know him. Uncle Fred was wonderful but reserved, and I didn't spend much time with him. But Andy was my hero, falling in a line of my heroes right after my dad. He was an amazing man and human being.

When Uncle Mark left Aunt Connie, Andy took on the role of father for my cousins Mary and Mark. He told everyone he had six kids, even though he had four. And he would have taken on my sister and myself without a blink of an eye and had eight kids. As a matter of fact, he would have loved it. He was a great man, father, and uncle to all of the cousins. He loved us all, and we knew it. There was no denying his genuine love and his big, beautiful heart. We lost him way too early to cancer.

He actually gave me my very first rose. I was a young girl of ten or eleven, and it was Easter morning. He had come home with Easter plants for Aunt Peggy and Aunt Connie. I was sitting in Peggy's kitchen drinking coffee. (They kind of let me do adult things, like smoke and drink coffee.) Andy came in with the Easter lilies and plants and then handed me that one red rose. I was tickled pink. He always had touched my heart and made me feel special and loved. That's just what he did.

Andy loved my aunt Peggy so much, and you could feel it every day, in every way. He was famous for his big breakfasts every Saturday and Sunday—pancakes, eggs, bacon, sausage, toast with lots of butter, anything you wanted. No one worried about cholesterol back then. He was equally famous for his mile-high lasagna, which he was in charge of making on holidays.

Peggy was and is tough as nails, but with a heart of gold as well. You knew she loved you, but she ruled with an iron fist. She never hit me that I can recall, but boy, could she scream and yell and curse. She also had a look that could stop you in your tracks, and when she gritted her teeth and spoke to you slowly, it was sometimes scarier than when she yelled. She had no patience for tears.

Growing up, I spent so many fun, interesting days and nights in that house. Most of them were as a silent observer of my aunts and grandmother. They spoke freely in front of me about everything from getting their period to childbirth to sex to family issues. I took it all in, learning at a young age about the divine feminine mystique. But of all my aunts, Ruby taught me the most about sex, love, and a little rock and roll. She was a flower child of the sixties and seventies, heavily laced with patchouli oil.

Back when I was really young, about six years old, my aunts were equally as young, and they lived at on Staten Island. I would sleep over there all the time. Ruby would take me out to hang out with her friends, but before we left, she would take out her stash of Marlboros, put a finger to her lips, stick the box cigarettes down her pants, and off we would go so she could smoke with her friends. Thinking back, I am absolutely sure they were smoking more than cigarettes.

This house was yet another place, of refuge even before I knew I needed one. I remember being in a big queen-size bed, crunched between Connie and Ruby, having late-night snacks. We would pass the jar of Fluff back and forth, sharing a spoon and sometimes dipping pretzels in Coca-Cola. I ate and drank until my stomach hurt.

But most of my craziest memories with Ruby took place at the crazy house in Brooklyn. Like the time she and her girlfriend decided to take me to the beach. *Great!* I thought. I loved the beach and was so excited that they wanted me to go with them. They were nineteen, and I was ten. To my utter horror, when we got there, I saw it was a completely nude beach. I do not remember being warned. I only remember the threat that I was not to tell a soul that they took me there.

There I saw my first penis, and it was not a pretty sight: an old, shriveled one. I almost fainted! The rest were all those of what appeared to be gay men with equally shriveled-looking things hanging from between their legs. The beach was all men, from what I can remember. Ruby and her friend took only their tops off, thank God. But I wanted to crawl under the sand and die a quick death.

I was so humiliated, I lay on the blanket for hours and hours with my visor down, reading my *Anne of Green Gables* book, so I could not see any more penises. I tried to lose myself in the story and forget where I was. When they were finally ready to leave, Ruby and her friend were talking about conversations they were going to have with their boyfriends later that night. They were saying things like, "Not tonight, honey," referring to their sunburned boobs.

In the back of my mind, after being around my aunt's candor for years, I thought I knew what that meant, but after the shriveled penis day, I really didn't ever want to know. That night I wound up as sick as a dog from sun poisoning. They hadn't given me sunscreen at the beach, and I never rolled over. So I burned!

I got to know my Aunt Ruby's boobs pretty well. She disliked wearing a bra—or a shirt, for that matter—so it wasn't unusual to be playing a game of Monopoly or Boggle when she would just rip off her shirt and bra and play the rest of the night topless. She slept only in her panties at night. So topless Aunt Ruby was very common.

I shared a bed with her many nights in the basement when my grandmother was out doing god knows what. More about that later. Ruby always went to bed with a glass of milk, a couple of Oreo cookies, and a glass of water. I think that's where my Oreo habit started—a habit I had and loved for about thirty-five years.

I remember one particular night hanging with Aunt Ruby in the basement, and a neighbor called to say that a car had hit Ruby's cat. It was a horrible scene. She screamed and cried. (Ruby was a big animal lover and loved her cat dearly.) When she finally calmed down, she put the cat in a shoebox and placed it on the bedroom dresser next to our bed. She took off her clothes, ate her Oreos, and passed out.

I did not sleep a wink. I watched that box all night long, positive the cat would come back to life and that any minute I would hear a meow and a little paw would knock the top off. I was beyond scared and could not wait for morning, when we would bury the cat in the backyard.

Chapter 4

Not Your Typical Granny

Growing up, I had the good fortune to have two grandmothers.

I never got to meet any of my grandfathers except my grandmother Lucia's second husband, Mike. He died when I was five, but I remember him fondly. He lived with my grandmother and my three youngest aunts, Connie, Peggy, and Ruby, at the house on Vince Avenue in Staten Island.

I spent a lot of time with Grandmother Lucia, whom I called Nanny. She was not your typical grandmother; she did not bake, knit, and take me to church or teach me to say my prayers, which I have heard other grandmas do.

She could sew, and I remember the big, old, black Singer sewing machine in the basement. Nanny was a seamstress with a few other odd jobs, like loan sharking and number running. Whenever my mom was sick or out of commission for one reason or another, I would become the ward of one of my many aunts or my grandmother, mostly.

Nanny didn't take me shopping or to the park, but she did take me places—like various apartments in Brooklyn and the occasional bar. She would have me sit at the end of the bar, and the bartender would feed me cherries and orange slices from his little set up for cocktails while she conducted her business.

Her other odd job was running numbers. People who worked for the numbers racket were called number runners. They collected bets from gamblers and delivered the payoff when the gamblers won. The final digits of the winning payoff results of horse races often determined the winning numbers. It is also true that when you compare the numbers game (which was an illegal lottery compared to today's legal state-controlled lottery), it did offer higher payoffs. Whether we were loan sharking or running numbers, I was generally riding shotgun with my grandmother, blissfully unaware.

Of course, at the time, I had absolutely no idea why I was sitting in a bar in my single-digit years being fed fruit cut for cocktails by a strange man. I did not even think about it. I thought it was normal. *This is what all kids do with their grandmothers, right?* Nope. They were knitting, baking, or church going. We were just doing a whole lot of riding around Brooklyn in the car all day and stopping off at bars and different apartments along the way. I guess you could say it was some form of education. It could have been worse. She could have been taking me into dark alleys, where there would be no fruit.

Chapter 5

The Garden Apartment—
Staten Island, New York

We moved into a garden apartment because the new house we were going to live in was not ready yet. I was nine. My parents thought it was perfectly okay to keep me in school at Mary of Faith School and had no problems with my taking the train by myself five towns and five train stops away in to get there.

The garden apartment building within walking reach of two different train station I would walk to the closest train station by myself and stand on the platform. It was an above ground station, which did not seem as scary to me, but I was still alone and frightened for all the reasons any little nine-year-old girl in fourth grade would be frightened about. I had a fear of someone snatching me; a fear of being alone; a fear of not knowing where I was going or if I would arrive there safe or at all; a fear of missing my stop and having to go back. All of those fears were present with me.

I remember the train pulling up, the smoke rising off the tracks, and the smell of coal and steel. I jumped into the train as soon as the doors opened, for fear of falling into the large crack between the train and the platform. I gave the conductor my twenty-five cents, and I asked him how many stops to my destination. Then I quickly settled into the scratchy wicker seats in my neatly pressed Catholic uniform with the high socks and little crisscross tie.

I looked around at the advertisements on the walls and the people hanging from the straps and just held my breath until I got to my stop. When the train stopped there, I got off and went up the stairs to the street. I turned left and started walking. I was so relieved that I cried when I saw my school.

I don't understand why Dad didn't just drive me those few towns to school. But he did eventually find two older kids that lived in our neighborhood who also went to Mary of Faith School. I would walk alone several blocks to their house, or sometimes get dropped off, and then take the train with them. I have no recollection of their names. We played a fun game where we would jump onto the tracks, leave a penny or nickel on the rail, and wait for the train to come by. Then we would jump back down and find our flattened treasure. Did my parents know or care that their nine-year-old daughter was jumping onto train tracks? Did the school know? How was this okay?

I never understood the logic (if you could call it that) of my parents. Why were we always moving? There seemed to be a good reason every time. Our little house was "bad luck," as I heard my grandmother say. What? It was a great neighborhood. The only one I knew. I had friends there. I liked my school. Why did we have to move to Oakdale? Why would you let a fourth-grader take the train by herself back to school? Was anyone in charge of me? They would not have even known if I got there. How did I eventually become the mother that followed her son's bus to school on the first day of kindergarten?

My memory of life in that apartment is kind of a blur. I didn't have to take the train for very long, because school was out before I knew it, which was probably the reason to keep me there instead of switching. I made friends with two sisters named Jennie and Annie, who lived around the corner and were the nieces of my mom's cousin Timmy. They were my lifesaver, and I don't know if they realized it. They had lost their mom and lived with their dad and two older siblings.

I hung out with Jennie and Annie all the time. I always slept over at their house, and I learned a lot from them. They taught me about cooking scrambled eggs, cleaning up a kitchen, and getting rid of pimples—which I did not have yet. When it came to cooking, I was fascinated by the way Jennie and Annie made scrambled eggs. I had never seen anything like it! They would crack the eggs and whisk them together with a fork as I had watched my mom do. But then they would open up the spice cabinet and proceed to put just about every spice and herb they could find into the eggs: a little oregano, parsley, basil, rosemary, garlic powder, black pepper, and salt. The eggs were delicious, and I made them that way myself any chance I got. I even wowed my grandmother Lucia with the creation one night. I asked if I could make myself scrambled eggs and if she wanted any. At first, she said no. But after seeing how I made them and smelling how delicious they were, she decided to join me.

By that time, my mom's Darvon addiction was getting worse. When we were being open and talking about her addiction, she admitted taking up to thirty pills a day to keep going. It was always a known fact in the house and in my family that she was probably lying. She was a habitual liar, and we all felt she was taking more. When we would come home to the apartment, it was not unusual to find her drunk. This is why I hardly went home.

I continued hanging out with Jennie and Annie, and sometimes my sister, my sister Andrea, would come with me. We swam in their pool, walked to the shopping center bargain store for little trinkets and treasures, and had many a slumber party at their house, talking long into the night. Their house seemed so much safer and more normal than mine.

I never wanted to be in our apartment, for obvious reasons. I know my mother was drinking then. But I don't remember it being really bad at that point. Something kept me out of that lonely apartment and away from her problems. This would be the start of finding refuge from the storm that was my life in many friends' homes.

Chapter 6

Fifth and Sixth Grade, Staten Island, New York

We were able to move into our new home in a few months. It was an older home—a beautiful English Tudor. I liked it there very much in the beginning. We had a little backyard with a cherry tree and an equally pretty front yard. The house was cozy, and I could feel the history. I hoped we'd live there forever and live happily every after. So far, it probably was the nicest home we had lived in.

The people who moved out left many treasures. I remember a really large collection of salt and pepper shakers. I am sure my mother gave them all away, as she did most things. There was also an old-fashioned telephone chair with a little desk attached to it. I still wonder where that went. My mother loved to be "like Santa Claus," as she put it—giving everything to people. She would give the shirt off her back. I think that was how she felt loved and appreciated and how she showed love when she was feeling okay.

My sister and I could have had our own rooms at the English Tudor house, but we chose to sleep together. Maybe we felt safer that way. Even though we were five years apart in age, we were very close and loved being together—when we weren't fighting, of course. I loved my sister with all my heart and really wanted to protect her from our lives, but I was too young and didn't know how. But my running away from my mother's craziness led me away from my sister. It saddens me to think of all the time we spent apart.

As I said, this house was special. There are some good memories laced with bad ones. It had a cute entranceway with a door that opened to a small vestibule as well as a wood-burning fireplace I remember hiding in when it was not lit. We lived there for only two very tumultuous years. It was a dark, lonely, and scary time.

When we first moved there, I was in the fifth grade, starting a new school again in September as the new girl at Our Lady Queen of Grace. Most of the kids had been together since kindergarten or first grade. Being the new kid is never fun, especially when going home is worse because there is no refuge. It makes a child feel constantly unsafe and on edge. *Why did my parents put me in yet another Catholic school in yet another town and drop me off at the train station again?* They didn't walk me inside or down to the track. They left me on the curb. *Figure it out, Tia.* I had so many scary times of being on trains by myself, trying to get to school, hoping I would get off at the right stop.

On my first day of fifth grade, my dad dropped me off at the train station. I got halfway down the stairs, sat on the steps, and put my face in my lap and cried. All I could see when I dared to open my eyes were men's and women's fancy shoes going up and down the stair on their way to work. Finally, a woman tapped me on the shoulders and said, "What's wrong?" and I replied, "I'm scared." She got me onto the right side of the tracks heading toward my new school and I was on my way to the first day of fifth grade at St. Mary of Hope School.

To make matters worse, my mother was really in the throes of her drinking and drugs. She had met one of my friends' mothers, who also drank, and they became drinking buddies—drinking screwdrivers in the afternoons and passing out by five o'clock at night.

Some nights were better than others. If Mom wasn't drinking, dinner was made, and maybe she would offer some help with homework, but that was not the norm. Dad was always there, trying to help and making excuses for my mom. It got so bad during those two years living on Brush Avenue that my aunts called Child Protective Services and wanted to take us away from my mom. I still have many questions about those years.

Mom continued to have grand mal epileptic seizures, which were still terrifying. One time, I was walking with my friends in a shopping center across from our home. I noticed my sister, Andrea, sitting in a shopping cart, screaming and crying outside the grocery store. When I rushed over, I looked inside the store and saw my mother on the floor, having a seizure. When I think of how frightened Andrea was, my heart breaks. And my heart also breaks for my poor mother lying on the floor. She must have been equally terrified.

That was the state that I vividly remember living in: fear. I was completely afraid to be alone with my own mother—the woman who was supposed to be my protector, comfort, shelter from the world.

I would beg my dad to take me with him when he left the house to run an errand or go to off-track betting. I loved going to off-track betting, picking horses and watching the races on TV in the smoke-filled room. It was even more fun when he won.

My favorite thing to do was to get a chocolate Italian ice, which was very popular in Staten Island and Brooklyn along with chocolate egg creams. About the only people who have heard of a chocolate egg cream grew up in Brooklyn. It's a beverage consisting of milk and soda water as well as vanilla or chocolate syrup. I'd never get the vanilla. There was also a guy with a little cart who sold Italian ice outside of the store from OTB.

Years later, that was the shopping center my mother shoplifted in and got caught. Why did she do it? I don't think we really needed anything she took. And I don't think it was for the money. When she shoplifted, we left the store, and security followed us out and escorted us back in. Police were called. I was so embarrassed and humiliated. My mother caused so much drama, and unfortunately, that would not be the last time she got arrested.

To be honest, I'm not even sure if it was the first time. She had a thing for stealing prescription pads at the doctor's office and writing her own scripts. She would drag my sister and me all over New York City in search of the next drug store that didn't know her, so she could fill her prescriptions.

Some of it is a little hazy, and there are so few people left to ask. I usually go to one of my mom's sisters, but they are all getting older, too. Sometimes I wonder how much they forget purposely or to protect my mother in some way. Denial is sometimes necessary when it's too painful to accept the truth.

In short, life in our little English Tudor had been a disaster, but it was full of memories. I shaved my legs for the first time in that house. I nearly shaved my eyebrows off and have the pictures to prove it. Didn't every girl do that?

I had my first real crush on a boy in the fifth grade, Charlie. He was the cutest. That started me on a lifelong pattern of crushes on short, dark, adorable, Italian guys. Charlie sang in the choir, and so did I. That's when I also started singing, but it was short-lived. My dad saw something in me and took me for voice lessons, but nothing came of it. My mother had no interest, as usual. I entered a few talent shows later with my best friend, Marianna Adamo, who was probably my first girl crush.

Chapter 7

Girlfriends

As far back as elementary school, one of my first girlfriends was Missy Sheridan, who took me under her wing in the first grade at Mary of Faith School and let me know I was okay. She was the youngest of five children in a big Irish family. I loved her house because it was big and old with doilies on the table and homemade crocheted blankets on the couches.

Her mom always greeted us after school with cookies and hot chocolate. Missy was the last of five; I think her parents had run out of bedrooms. I was intrigued by her bedroom, but I understand now that it was probably the nursery. You had to walk through her parents' large master bedroom to get to the door to Missy's room. It was very girly and pink with lace curtains decorating crank-out leaded-glass windows. I loved having dinner with them and sleeping over. They always ate at the dining-room table. We passed around big bowls of meat and potatoes, and everything tasted wonderful. There was always dessert and always a fire in the fireplace in the wintertime.

The one and only time Missy came over to my house for a sleepover was a nightmare. She left before the night was over because my mom went into some kind of rage about a mess we made in the basement. I can't recall much more than that and Missy wanting to go home. We were only in the third grade, and perhaps she did not want to be away from home, but I'm pretty sure to this day it had something to do with Mom flying off the handle. I was humiliated. I had started learning at a young age that it was best not to have sleepovers at my house because I never knew what would happen, and ultimately, it would not be good.

I met most of my tribe in the first semester of fifth grade at St Mary of Hope School. They soon became my refuge from home.

The first girlfriend in fifth grade was my lifelong friend, Marianna Adamo. It was love at first sight. Marianna was the popular, pretty girl. She was probably the prettiest girl in fifth grade with the biggest brown eyes and longest eyelashes I had ever seen. She lived right around the corner from school, and it was not long before she started inviting me to her house after school, which I loved. Marianna sold Chiclets out of her uniform pockets for five cents and would later become one of the youngest Avon saleswomen. She was always wearing Avon perfume pins. She had one for every season and reason you could think of. Marianna accepted me right away as her friend. I didn't even have to try; it just came naturally. She was and is to this day one of the sweetest, kindest people I know.

Marianna's best friend was Jennifer, She was also very kind and very friendly and made me feel accepted right away. Jennifer had an older sister, Mary, who was two grades above us and was a real tough Cookie. You did not want to mess with Mary. Deep down, Mary was a sweetheart. Jennifer and I would come in and out of each other's lives as we got older, but she always did and always will hold a special place in my heart.

I also came to know Carol Falco, Laura Rizzo, Laura Marino and Holly Smith, as the semester went on. They were a little tribe unto themselves. They lived near each other and all walked home together. They had all been friends since kindergarten or first grade.

It turned out that Laura Rizzo's dad and my dad were friends from the old neighborhood in Brooklyn. Laura was also one of the prettiest girls, with long, jet-black hair and gorgeous big brown eyes. She was also kind and accepting. Laura had an older sister and a younger sister and brother.

Carol Falco was a beautiful girl with a heart of gold and long, brown hair and brown eyes. I spent a lot of time with the Falco family, eating dinner with them many nights, sleeping over just as many nights, and feeling very happy when I was there. Mrs. Falco was really wonderful to me. She crocheted homemade blankets for me and even came out to see me in the hospital when I had mono, bringing a strawberry JELL-O dish in a Tupperware mold.

Carol's parents would take off for Florida a few times a year and leave her older brother, Lenny, in charge of us. Well, Lenny let us do just about anything we wanted to do. We had many parties there with lots of underage drinking. There was late-night swimming and all-day sun-tanning sessions while smoking cigarettes and slathering ourselves with baby oil laced with iodine. Somehow we survived it all. Carol is very dear to my heart and always will be.

Holly Smith was and is a sweetheart of a girl with a gorgeous heart. I didn't spend as much time over at her house, but when I did, it was epic. One time we decided to pierce her ears, and I had the brilliant idea to use the largest, thickest needle in her mom's sewing kit to make it go faster. Needless to say, it was almost a disaster. But I got it in there and got that ear pierced. Another memory was the night of the big New York City blackout in 1977. Her parents were away, and my dad wouldn't come to get me because there was not so much as a stoplight or streetlight. We were terrified because it was also the summer of the Son of Sam.

Next, I met Serena, and I will talk more about her later. Her mom, Sunny, took me in for most of my senior year of high school. I met Serena on the first day of sixth grade as the new girl again at another new school. We became fast friends, and I thank God I met her.

Eventually, I would meet Deb at yet another new school for seventh grade. Deb was another earth angel that took me under her wing and accepted me, the new girl. She was one of the "rich" girls from the private school I went to later on. We rode the private bus together, but she was kind and sweet, and like most of my friends, she was short and Italian, with brown hair and brown eyes. She was so accepting of me and loved me like a sister.

We loved Elton John and David Bowie and knew all the words to the *Yellow Brick Road* and *Ziggy Stardust* albums. She became a refuge for me just like the rest of my tribe. I lost track of her after high school, but thanks to the magic of Facebook, we reconnected. I was so happy to see that she had married a wonderful, caring man that adores her and that they have two beautiful children. We've remained friends, and we have a friendship I treasure.

I slept over at my girlfriends' houses more than they did mine because I was always worried about the scene at my house. We never knew what could happen. I wondered, *Will my mom be drunk or stoned?* And I answered myself, *Probably.* I just couldn't take that risk. And I remembered what had happened with Missy.

So I stayed at Marianna's house a lot growing up, and her mom would stuff us with food. Marianna's mom, Mrs. Adamo ("Mrs. A"), was a character. I would take a cab, or my dad would drive, or sometimes Mrs. A would pick me up and drop me off. She was the best. Not to go off on a tangent about her, but she seemed to be what moms are supposed to be. She was ahead of the times when it came to health and wellness, Mrs. A had a "no smoking" sign on her kitchen fridge in 1971 when I first met her. This was a time when it was all the rage to smoke, and there weren't warnings on cigarette packs yet. My parents smoked in the house. Heck, they smoked in the car with us in the backseat with the windows rolled up!

Marianna and I started smoking when we were in fifth grade, although I think I had my very first cigarette at a younger age, probably during the Garden Apartment days. One time, we thought we could outsmart her mom and smoke in her room. We opened the windows and dragged the vacuum cleaner into the room, turned it on, lit up, and blew our smoke into the suction of the vacuum cleaner. That lasted all of five minutes before she smelled the smoke and started screaming. Of course, we told her that she was crazy and that we were absolutely not smoking.

I loved going to Marianna's house because Mrs. A always made dinner every night. She cooked mostly from scratch. She would talk about things like eating whole foods for better nutrition and getting your vitamin C from a real orange, not a pill. Each night of the week, dinner was always the same, except on Tuesday and Thursday. Those two days could vary. The menu went like this: soup on Monday was either lentil, chicken, or vegetable (the Italian belly wash after the big Sunday meal); meatloaf on Tuesday; chicken cutlet on Wednesday; Prince Spaghetti day, Thursday was hamburgers; fish on Friday (because, as catholic's we would never eat meat on Friday").

Sometimes they had pizza on a Friday, too. Saturdays was steak night ; and of course, macaroni was on Sunday. (In case you're wondering, we didn't call it pasta growing up. It was macaroni, no matter if it was spaghetti, ziti, or linguini.)

My mother was a waitress all over Staten Island. I think she worked in every diner. She enjoyed it and would come home with wads of ones and fives from her tips. Breakfast was whatever you wanted. Most morning I had Oreos and milk or Ring Dings or Devil Dogs or coffee cake. You could say mornings were made by Nabisco and Drake's Cakes. I was given money to buy lunch at school, or we'd make baloney sandwiches or hot dogs with beans for lunch. Something my sister and I would make breakfast for dinner, like eggs or pancakes or French toast.

When I was home, my mom did cook—if she was doing well. I can remember a few things she made, like brisket of beef. The brisket was made with a packet of Lipton's onion soup and a can of Campbell's cream of mushroom soup. Most families were probably cooking that way in the seventies. Brisket was her specialty, besides Sunday sauce made with meatballs, sausage, and pork braciola. *Delicious.* I don't and would never eat meat today, but I remember how good that was. My sister and I would also have Campbell's alphabet soup for lunch all the time. We would have a little contest every time we ate it. We would take out the lima beans as we found them and place them on the rim of the bowl. Whoever had the most lima beans was the winner.

Marianna lived around the corner from school, so her house made a convenient after-school hangout spot. Mrs. A (who did not drink at all) always had fresh-baked goodies waiting, such as her infamous raspberry butter thumbprint cookies. I'm salivating as I write. They were the most delectable cookies ever. Her cookies were to die for, and I still make them at Christmas time. She was also known for her chocolate mayonnaise cake and her pistachio cake. They were not works of art like today's cakes; they were simple, homemade, and incredibly moist and delicious.

Marianna's home was a home of comfort and looked like a lot of homes on TV did in the seventies: plastic on the couches, one TV in the living room, one phone in the kitchen with a very long cord so you could lock yourself in the bathroom with it. It was different from my house in one main way: it was not scary. You always knew what you were going to get when you got home.

Mrs. A was a little crazy in her own way, but so sweet and giving, which is why Marianna is as sweet as she is. She always locked the front door behind you as soon as you walked in. She was consistent with being home when you got home, consistent with meals, consistent with baking, and consistent with her green tube of Revlon Moon Drops lipstick. The shade was called "I Love Pink," and she would not leave the house without applying it. That is what I loved about going to Marianna's house: consistency. You knew what was around every corner, be it her grumpy dad, Mr. A; her sister, Mary Ann; or her Basset hound, Babs.

Unlike any one of my many homes, Marianna lived in that house her entire life, and her mom still lives there today. When I go back to her house now, it's as if I never left forty years ago—same rugs, same couches, same everything. It's like a shrine to the 1970s, and I love it. It still has Mrs. A's vegetable garden in the side yard. Every dog they ever had was buried in the yard. Marianna's childhood room is pretty much the way she left it.

As an adult, I hear friends say that to this day they never sleep as well as when they go home. I never had that opportunity. I got to go home once or twice to my parents' condo, which was the last home either of my parents lived in. My father died on the corner of that street. My mother declined to her death at that address, so when I had to go back there to sleep, it was not pleasant and certainly not my best night of sleep.

I realize I had always sought refuge. Thinking back on my life, I know there was always that one girlfriend. No matter which house I lived in or which school I went to, I was blessed with a girlfriend/angel that let me know I was okay. I was loved, and they had my back. I could sleep at their house and have dinner with them. I could escape from the reality of what was happening at home.

After a half-year of fifth grade at St. Mary of Hope School, my parents decided after the holidays that Catholic school wasn't necessary (or maybe they didn't want to pay the tuition). Beginning in the New Year, I went to the local public school. I walked there and back by myself everyday, scared, and did not make any real friends there.

When I got to the classroom on the first day of school, I met my teacher, Mr. Dugger, who became one of my favorite teachers. I came to find out that they had sex education, something they certainly were not teaching in Catholic school. God forbid! My parents had to sign a permission slip for me to take part in that class. Thank goodness they did because it seemed like only a few nerdy kids were not allowed to, and I was having a hard enough time fitting in as the new girl.

Before the first sex-ed class ended, we had a quiz. I failed miserably because I knew nothing from a penis to a fallopian tube. *Sperm? What the heck are they talking about?* I remember Mr. Dugger getting a chuckle from some of my answers because they were so wrong they were funny.

I have to say, everything I know about sex and the reproductive system and how to make a baby I learned in that class. It was a game changer. I now understood that there really was not a stork and that, yes, in some way God is responsible for getting a baby in a mommy's belly. I was surprised because there was a lot more going on behind the scenes. It was fascinating and creepy all at the same time for a ten-year-old. My mom never sat me down and had "The Talk" with me about the birds and bees. Truthfully, she didn't have to because I learned it all in Mr. Dugger's class in the second half of the fifth grade—all the while having my first crush on the most adorable boy.

Although I switched schools, I still stayed friends with my St. Mary of Hope girls. Like all young girls, we would stay up late at Marianna's house and talk about boys. We'd go into the bathroom and put on all the makeup we found in her mother's drawers. Mrs. A would always wake up because of our giggling in that tiny bathroom or Marianna's little room. The houses built back in the sixties in Staten Island were all on forty-by-forty lots, and the houses were no more than about two thousand square feet. So the bedrooms and bathrooms were all within a whisper's distance— and whisper we did, long into the night and early-morning hours. We plotted our lives and spent hours dreaming of the days when we could have a boyfriend, travel, and be of age to smoke, drink, and wear makeup.

I went on to attend many different schools, but the girls stayed and eventually graduated from St Mary of Hope. We always were close friends, seeing each other on weekends and having sleepovers. We had many a boyfriend, went to school dances and sleep-away camp together, and stayed out later than we should have.

It was at sleep-away camp, that I would meet one of my other earth angel friends, Erin Ford. She was and still is the sweetest and most loyal friend you could ask for. I met her at camp with Marianna, and we all became best friends. She lived in Pennsylvania, and had the cutest accent compared to our New York way of speaking.

We spent at least five years going to camp, from age nine to fourteen or so. Even when camp was over, we were together. Marianna and I would take the bus from Penn Station to Pennsylvania, and Erin would sometimes take the bus to see us. Her mom had a pure heart and was so lovely. She also stuffed us with food like Mrs. A and always had fresh-baked Cookies and brownies for us, plus three meals a day that she made from scratch. Her home was cozy and warm, and it was another place of refuge.

It's a miracle how we stayed together. My little Staten Island tribe all lived in the same town, most within walking distance of each other. Even after my move to Astronaut Avenue, I hung out with them in the summer almost every night. I managed to stay with them, no matter what. Whatever I had to do to get to my friends, I did. I would take cabs, buses, and trains. Sometimes my dad drove me, and sometimes the girls' moms or dads picked me up or dropped me off back home. I think everyone's parents knew I needed some TLC—especially Carol and Marianna's family.

Chapter 8

Astronaut Avenue, Staten Island, New York

I spent sixth grade at a new public school. We had moved again, from our pretty English Tudor to an apartment on Astronaut Avenue in a small community in Staten Island. Ours was a quaint little development with streets named after astronauts. Sounds nice enough, right? But it was not nice in any way shape or form. It was hell.

I had a few theories on why we moved: Money problems. More bad luck. My parents marriage was on the rocks.

My mom never drove, having come from the city and being epileptic. Thank God! She would have surely killed someone or herself. I could just picture her getting in the car drunk and doing who knows what. So epilepsy was a blessing in disguise. Though she couldn't drive, she was determined to get around. So she took cabs and buses and trains everywhere to get her Darvon and alcohol. As usual, my sister and I spent many a day on the trains with my mom, going from borough to borough, while she tried to get pills from different drugstores.

My mom's stays in and out of hospitals were for long periods—weeks, sometimes a month. They were long and lonely times. I spent so much time in hospitals visiting my mom growing up that they freak me out. I can visit for a short period before I start getting anxious as memories flood back. I think about the many times I had to sit and watch my mom suffer in a hospital bed.

I think my dad had been planning on leaving for quite some time. I don't think he could take it anymore, living with my mom and her addictions. I'm pretty sure that selling the house on Brush Avenue and moving to the Astronaut Avenue apartment was part of a plan for him to leave. He stayed with us there for a very short period before he moved out. He returned after my mom's heart attack years later.

Many fights and crazy things happened while we lived on Astronaut Avenue. Dad would get so mad at Mom when he'd come home and find her drunk. But you can't argue with a drunk; many times he did until she went to her room and to bed to sleep it off. I would sometimes confide with my sister. We would always talk ourselves to sleep at night by playing games like who could come up with the most names that began with each letter of the alphabet. When I got older, I was more likely to be under the covers, on my phone with a boyfriend, or with a girlfriend who was also sneaking a call.

Mom's rage was scary. She would scream at us at the top of her lungs, curse at us, and jump up and down. I remember her getting red in the face and throwing things around. It was not unlikely for her to pick up a glass she was drinking from or pick up anything she could grab hold of and throw it at one of us. She would also pick up a brush or wooden spoon and chase one of us around the house until she caught that person and let her have it. I remember one time my room was a mess, and she came in and flung everything off my dresser with one big whoosh, breaking most of my things. She did not care. The only thing you could do was stand there, cry, and say you were sorry for whatever set her off.

My father didn't actually leave my mom right after we moved there. I think he stayed on for my sister and me. Someone had to try to make some sense out of our days. But eventually, he gave up. He moved out and separated from Mom. As a result, they decided I needed to go back to Catholic school, though I don't know how they afforded it. So off I went to St. Marks Villa Academy, on a private bus that picked up rich kids, which I was not at all. I was picked up from my second-floor garden apartment that I shared with my sister, my usually unstable mother, and some of the time, my father. We drove through all the rich neighborhoods in Staten Island, picking of wealthy, somewhat snobby kids, from their large home in the wealthy communities.

So I found myself in a private Catholic school run by nuns and surrounded by wealthy girls and boys that had better clothes, better parents, and better hair. It was a tough time being the new girl going through puberty. I remember being bullied on the bus for my pimples and frizzy hair and not having the best coat or hat. It's the way it went every day. But that's when I met my lifelong friend, Deb, who became part of my tribe.

Thank God for the school uniform because that saved me from the fact that my wardrobe was less than complete. I didn't have the kind of mother that took her daughter shopping. I remember once in the sixth grade, while in public school, crying to my dad about my clothes, which were mostly hand-me-downs from my older cousin Amanda I was so ashamed and humiliated by the way I was dressed. Everyone else was wearing jeans and cool clothes. Does anyone remember Danskin clothes? Ugh. I'm not talking about the cool Danskin line that was popular with dancers and disco-goers in the eighties. I'm talking about the same material made into pants and shirts in ugly orange colors. Those were my hand-me-downs: polyester dorky clothes that my mom thought were the best possible clothing any young girl could want to wear.

I hated it! So, my dad felt bad and took me shopping. I remember that shopping spree so vividly. I was so happy to be buying jeans and cool tops and a new pair of shoes. No wonder to this day I still have trouble dressing, although I have wonderful friends who are happy to help. And I am getting better at it.

One thing Mom got real good at around the time Dad left her was shoplifting. If that woman had put her energy into something useful and sobered up, she could have run a small country. These were not fun times; they were embarrassing times, especially when she was caught. And she got caught at least two times when I was with her.

The few times I actually went shopping with my mom during those times I didn't realize she was shoplifting—until one night. We were with her friend Carol and were heading back to the car when she was stopped in the parking lot by a security guard. He took her inside to a back office, and I waited with Carol. I was scared, very embarrassed, and wondered once again what would happen to my mom.

Will she go to jail? Will I ever see her again? These were the same scary thoughts that came up for me over and over in my childhood. *Is she going to have a seizure? Will she die?* Drunk on the floor. *Will she wake up? Will she be okay? Will I be okay?* Getting arrested. *Will she come home?* And sometimes she was just plain old missing. *Where's Mom? Who knows. Will someone bring her home drunk? Will she arrive home drunk and bloody and muddy from falling outside? Or will the phone ring because someone found her somewhere and managed to get her phone number out of her?* Sometimes she just took off wandering. She was just a mess—a lost soul.

She tried 12 step programs but never quite got that right. I was a veteran twelve-stepper myself. I didn't have much of a choice. I would go with my mom to her twelve-step meeting and downstairs was the children and teenager meeting. It was helpful, but I had a hard time sharing and opening up to the group. I remember walking into the room, which was smoke filled and noisy. The meetings usually took place in a church basement. There was always a big pot of coffee and lots of donuts and Cookies. (I think that's where I got my love for jelly donuts.)

My mom's 12 step friends were nice people. Even the guy she rented her room out to was nice, but I was scared having him in the house. He was a stranger. What the hell was she thinking to have a strange man living in the house with her two young daughters? Nothing ever happened, but it could have.

I can remember my mom reaching certain goals, like ninety meetings in ninety days. But I'm not sure if she was honest. I'm not sure if she was still drinking or taking Darvon. I eventually graduated to every 12- step group there was for family members. Right into adult hood, going to meetings for adult children of alcoholics. Everything was helpful especially knowing I was not the only one feeling the way I did and understanding where insecurities and fears are born. Growing up with that kind of constant stress is unbearable at times. Constantly waiting for the other shoe to drop—or your mother to drop—is awful.

To this day, no matter where I am, whether in my home or in public, when I hear a loud bang or feel the floor shake, I jump. A little part of me remembers running to see what happened. *Is she having a seizure? Is she passed out? Did she fall? Maybe it's a heart attack.* I was always on that edge of fear. It would take me years to understand the anxiety especially after I started having anxiety attacks in my late twenties. I had to learn to breathe again. Through meditation and prayer and lots and lots of therapy, I learned to heal and find moments of peace.

We lived in the apartment on Astronaut Avenue for ten years. That was the longest I ever lived anywhere, in that sad second-floor apartment with few happy memories. That was my home. That's where we stayed for ten years? Talk about bad luck. Through my four years in high school, it was a living hell. My father tried to break free and have a life. Most people judge him for that. They think he was wrong. They say he abandoned my sister and me.

Even my mother's own sisters went through periods of not talking to her. They needed a break from her craziness.

Later on, as an adult, I had one therapist try hard to make me angry with my dad. She wanted me to take him off the pedestal I had him on. But I still give him a pass. I know where he came from. When you know better, you do better, and he did the best he could with what he knew. There, I said it!

Dad married Mom when he was twenty years old because she was pregnant and he loved her. No matter where he was, he was always a phone call away. I knew I could call him morning, noon, or night, and he would drop whatever he was doing and be at my side. And this was long before cell phones.

By the time St. Mark's Villa was over and it was time for high school, I decided I had to be with my girls. They were all going to a local public high school. I enrolled using a fake address of my dad's friend, Jim Kelley, lived near the school I wanted to attend. Living on Astronaut Avenue and commuting to the other side of the Island was no easy task. Two city buses, a transfer, and making sure I had enough change was a daily routine. I never knew anyone on the first bus, and it was lonely and boring.

I became best friends with Jim's daughter, Diane, and stayed there many nights. We had to take only one bus from her house because she was only a few towns away from school. Diane and I would always run into friends during the commute, compare nail polish and lipstick, and laugh a lot. I spent a lot of time on buses and trains, and it was worth it to be with my girlfriends.

I did not like school. I had no direction. My friends and I lied about staying over at each other's houses when we were really sleeping under the bleachers at school or driving to Pennsylvania to see boys that we met in Wildwood one summer. There were so many trips down to Wildwood, so many nights out dancing till we dropped. Marianna was the ringleader, and we all basically went along with anything she cooked up.

One of our favorite things to do was to sleep on the beach. God help us, I don't know how we survived. We would come home from a night of dancing and drinking and put on our bathing suits, get our chairs, and walk to the beach by the moonlight. We would fall asleep laughing and wake up surrounded by kids and families and ice cream vendors ringing their bells. We had so much fun.

I thank God for bringing these girls into my life. I don't know what I would have done without them. I feel truly blessed that our lives and hearts crossed. I can't put a finger on whatever it was that bonded us, but that bond still holds true today.

When I was in my teens, I practically lived back in Brooklyn at the crazy house, with the rest of my family. Whole summers. Easter breaks. Christmas breaks. Whenever I could, I retreated back over the bridge to escape my mother and the craziness at home.

Some nights I'd find myself on Serena's couch in Staten Island, if it was a school night. After everyone went to bed, I'd cry myself to sleep. I was so scared and so lonely. I felt very fractured from my family. My mom was very sick and usually in the hospital during my teen years. I'd lay there and ask. *Where is my mom at this moment? Does she wonder where or how I am? Where is my sister?* Dad worked nights around that time, resurfacing the streets, bridges, and byways of New York City. I was terrified some nights, consumed with panic over where my family's life was going.

I never spoke to anyone about it. I would wake up in the morning my usual self and go about my day. I don't think I ever told anyone what went on in my home or in my mind, even all the nights my mom was drunk or an ambulance was called because she was incoherent. I just went to school the next day and acted like every other kid.

What does that say about a young girl? I guess it was about keeping secrets, but no one ever told me not to tell. I kept my secrets anyway, acted normal, and held it all inside. I would say to myself, "I'm going to put that in the back of my head and never think about it again." And I prayed for better days.

Looking back, I realize I was always running in the other direction of my home. I could get away with anything because my father was too busy working and my mom was too busy drinking and drugging. For most of my teenage years, Dad did not live with us, so it was pretty much a free-for-all. I did some stupid stuff like teens sometimes do, but for the most part, I was a good kid. God and his angels were always watching over me.

My friends and I smoked pot and cut class, and since I got to the mailbox first, I could easily swipe the absentee letters the school sent; so no one ever saw them. I would also swipe my report cards, sign them myself, and return them to my teachers. It was easy because no one asked. (Actually, eventually someone asked, but I got around it. My answers were accepted, and I was never questioned again.)

Girls just want to have fun, so I went to the clubs at night to dance, even when I was way too young. I don't know how I got into the bars and clubs from the time I was fourteen, but I did. I didn't even drink. Who had money? I went dancing and had fun with my friends. Eventually, my high school caught up with me and decided it would be best if I did a work-to-school program. I worked a week and went to school a week. I loved it! I had no school every other week, and I got to dress up and go into New York City to make work and money.

Most of my senior year, I lived with my girlfriend Serena; her mom, Sunny; her sister, Roxanne; and her younger brother, Billy. At that time, depending on if I slept at home or at Serena's house, I took the train to the ferry. I loved the ferry because it was the cheapest form of transportation at that time. The Staten Island Transit cost fifty cents, and the ferry was a quarter. If I slept at home, I had to take the city bus that cost $2.50, which was a lot of money to me in those days.

So I worked and played and shopped in the city. On my lunch breaks and after work, I'd hit the shops down town and buy clothes and shoes for work. The Financial District had tons of shopping, and I couldn't wait to spend my earnings.

There was nothing terrible about living at Serena's. As a matter of fact, it was a lot of fun most times. Sunny was a single parent. She was pretty lenient, and she was out quite a bit with her boyfriend. We basically had free run of the apartment and our own agenda on most nights.

Sunny was very good to me. She cooked delicious meals for us and even made special food for me when I got sick with gastritis that year. No wonder my stomach was in knots; there was way too much chaos for me at home. Doctors put me on something to relax my stomach and a bland diet. Sunny took care of me and was yet another surrogate mother. She made me poached eggs and pastina and anything the doctors said would be beneficial.

I will be eternally grateful for all she did for me and for everything she taught me. She advised me on what to order at a restaurant on my first real date. I was going out with a boy named Frank. I was very worried about eating in front of a boy. Sunny told me to order the chicken marsala and cut it up into little pieces. "You will be fine," she said. I was, and I used that dish as my go-to dinner many times on many different dates.

Sunny also took me shopping for my prom dress. She was very fashionable. So while all the other girls were in long, chiffon, boring gowns, I wore a tasteful, electric blue jumpsuit with spaghetti straps and a cinched waist. It was incredible. She also sat me out by the pool to get a tan before the event. I looked and felt amazing. I eventually graduated high school out of that apartment in Ray Terrace, too. My dad and sister picked me up, and we drove to my High School. Afterward we went to the local restaurant for dinner.

The nightmare that was Astronaut Avenue culminated with my mom having a heart attack and my dad moving back in with us. It wasn't to be a husband but to be a friend and support to my mom and to be there for my sister and me. My mother had started cleaning houses at one point for a doctor on Staten Island. One day, when she was running an errand for the doctor, she began to have chest pain. She brought herself to the ER, and I got the call that she was there. I thought it was just another visit to the hospital.

Over the course of my life, I had visited many a hospital to see my mom. Hospitals, psych wards, nursing homes—you name it, she wound up there. When I got to the hospital, I saw my mother in the ER with an oxygen mask. The doctor took me aside and told me that she was having a massive heart attack. The years of drinking and drugging were finally getting to her at only age forty. My dad arrived shortly after I did. Next, of course, was my grandmother, then my aunts and uncles. Mom was not doing well and was transferred to the Cardiac Care Unit.

The family was solemn and worried. Mom was hooked up to machines and on oxygen; she was not speaking at that point because she was heavily sedated. I was scared, worried, and anxious, wondering if this would be the time she died. I had wondered that so many times in my life, and so I went to the hospital chapel and once again went into a bidding war with God. *If you save her this time, God, I'll do anything. Go back to church, stop smoking, never swear, and be nicer to my sister. Anything, just please do not let her die.*

It was a scary night and few days. After visiting her, I went to see Frank my boyfriend at the time. He lived in an apartment not far from ours. I got there wanting to be hugged and consoled; once again, it seemed for sure that she would die. But I realized that Frank wasn't capable of consoling me. While I sat and cried, he seemed confused. He made jokes to try to lighten up the mood, but that only made me feel worse. Our two-year relationship had run its course.

Mom didn't die, but my relationship with Frank was over. She recovered, but her heart had some damage. I swear that woman had nine lives, and she was taking a few of mine with her.

Soon after my mom's heart attack, I went to Frank's apartment to break it off. He was not happy about it at all. He begged me not to do it. At one point he went outside for something. When he came back in, we continued arguing about breaking up. I said I'd had enough and went outside to leave. When I got in my car, it would not start. I finally called my dad, who came over. He took a look under the hood and rang Frank's doorbell. Evidently, he had taken the starter wire off the engine so I couldn't leave. My father knew his way around a car engine.

With all my romantic relationships, I was the one to end them. Over time it seemed like I dated or married the wrong guy for whatever reason and then suddenly woke up and ended it.

Part Two

She
Is clothed in
Strength
and
Dignity,
she can
Laugh
Without fear
Of the future

Proverbs 31:25

Peas and Macaroni

Ingredients:
   1 medium onion, diced
   2 cloves garlic, minced
   1 teaspoon dried basil or 5 fresh leaves, chopped
   1 28-ounce can crushed tomatoes
   1 can peas
   Salt and pepper, to taste
   Pinch of crushed red pepper flakes
   1pound small shell pasta
   Extra virgin olive oil

Directions:
   Sauté onion and garlic in extra-virgin olive oil until soft. Add crushed pepper and dried or frozen basil (if using). Add tomatoes, salt, black pepper. Let cook for about 25-30 minutes. Add peas. (This should be a loose sauce but not soupy. Use as much or as little liquid as you like. If using frozen peas, add some of the starchy pasta water to thin out the sauce.)

   Let cook for another 10 or 15 minutes on low to combine flavor of peas with sauce.

   Meanwhile, cook pasta in salted boiling water until al dente. Toss pasta with sauce, adding more pasta water if it's too thick. Top with grated cheese. Enjoy!

Pasta Fagiolo

Ingredients:
    1 15-ounce can cannellini beans, do not drain or rinse
    2 cloves garlic, minced
    2 tablespoons olive oil
    Salt and pepper to taste
    1 pound elbow macaroni

Directions:
    Sauté garlic in olive oil; do not brown. Add in beans and juice from can. Toss with cooked macaroni. You can add a bit more olive oil if sauce is dry. Enjoy!

Mom's Cheesecake

Ingredients:
    4 16-ounce containers cream cheese
    2 16-ounce containers sour cream
    2 cups of sugar
    6 eggs
    1 tablespoons vanilla

Directions: Preheat oven to 350
    Blend all ingredients together and place into graham cracker crust. Bake for 50 minutes or, until center is almost set. Run a knife around the rim of the pan to loosen cake; cool before removing and rim completely. Refrigerate cheesecake for at least 4 hours before serving.

Crust

Ingredients:

 6 1/2 ounces graham crackers (12 crackers), finely ground
 (1 1/2 cups)
 2 1/2 ounces (5 tablespoons) unsalted butter, melted
 1/4 cup sugar
 1/3 teaspoon salt

Directions:

 Combine all ingredients with a fork. Firmly press crumb mixture into bottom and up sides of a 9-inch spring-form pan. Bake until crust is fragrant and edges are golden, 12-14 minutes. Let cool completely on wire rack. You can top with canned cherries or crushed pineapple.

Chapter 9

The Good The Bad and The Ugly, Staten Island, New York

W hen I met my husband, Michael, I did not have a clue as to who I was: a wounded twenty-year-old girl who'd never had a chance to catch her breath.

After Frank, I dated a few different guys. His friends wanted to date me. Please, really? I wanted nothing long-term after him. I did date a guy I met at work. He was a nice guy, but not my type. It ended quickly. At the time I worked in the court house processing new arrests.

I loved my job there. It was so much fun, and there was never a dull moment. I worked in the new-arrest processing office. I sat across from one of the young attorney's while the police officer told him about the arrest, and the attorney read out loud to me the legal terms for the docket. I typed away while they gave me all the information about the crime. I met many, many young police officers when I worked there. I was pretty, bubbly, and did *not* want to date a cop.

My reasoning was that if I started dating a cop here and there, I could get a reputation. Most of them were worse than washwomen when it came to gossip, and I didn't want anyone making up stories about me and passing them around. I didn't even want a boyfriend at the time. I was having a blast being single. It was 1981, and all I wanted to do was go out with my girlfriends, clubbing, dancing, and drinking the night away. I was having fun.

That's right around the time Michael walked into my office, and soon enough, my life changed, and in many ways for the better. It was his first arrest as police officer, and I helped with the process.

When we met, I was not even interested in dating him. But he was very persistent on going out with me, so I finally said yes to a date. It was the eighties, so of course I got dressed up. I teased and sprayed my hair as big as it could get, put on my heels and red lipstick, and waited for him to arrive. He showed up in jeans, a sweatshirt, and sneakers and took me to his house to meet his parents and watch Monday night football. Really? Did I mention I'm not a football fan?

But believe it or not, there was something there. I saw the way he treated his mom. He showed me all the pretty collections she had and all the different pieces he had bought her as gifts. I could see he was a good guy who loved his family. We started dating that night, and that was it. Six months later, he asked me to marry him, and I said yes. Just. Like. That.

I was only twenty-one—a child who knew nothing about her self. But I loved him in the way I understood love at that time.

I know now after years of sitting in therapy that I sought refuge in Michael and his family and their kindness. They were and are good people who loved and accepted me unconditionally. I needed to be rescued, and he rescued me from my crazy life. I did not see it then, but he was a way out. He was a chance to get away from my mother and to distance myself from her dysfunction and the daily pain I was living in.

So we got married on the unusually sweltering day in the fall of 1985. Marianna was there, of course; she was the first person to get to my house. Our friend Tina, came over and did our makeup, and we got ready for the big day. My dad walked me down the aisle and gave his baby girl away. It was all picture-perfect.

I had a beautiful wedding, but I felt dead inside. I was a bride just going through the motions. My mother managed to get drunk, but at least she waited until the end of the night. She still ruined the wedding in my mind, but it didn't matter. In my heart of hearts, I wasn't there. I was a shell—a walking, breathing, laughing, beautiful shell of a girl. My heart knew I had made a mistake very early on, but I did not know what to do about it.

Michael and I moved into our first little house together on Staten Island. I was so happy, *finally* after all those years of taking buses and cabs to see my friends. I was now living in the same town as all of my friends, and that warmed my heart immensely. My little house and my life with Michael felt safe. We settled in, and I enjoyed being a wife and playing house. It was a relatively calm time during the first year. I had no idea what storms were on the horizon.

Of course, my mother was always up to her old tricks, but that was life as we knew it. It just was the way it was. I was very codependent. My life revolved around when my mom was having a good or bad day. If I called her, and she was drunk and high, I had a bad day. If she sounded relatively happy and sober, I could go on to have a good day. There were still times she went missing because she had a fight with my dad, and we would find her holed up at the local Holiday Inn. Eventually, she would sober up and go home until the next time.

Within a year after our first wedding anniversary, the worst, most unthinkable nightmare happened. It was October in 1986. Michael and I had been married a little over a year. I was sitting in my living room, watching my favorite show at the time, *Hotel*, with Michael and Marianna, who lived around the corner at her mom's house. Someone was run over on the show, and I remember saying, "Oh wow, I felt that." I also had a weird feeling. It was just like any other Wednesday night before the phone rang around ten.

The caller was my sister, saying that dad had been in a car accident on the corner of our block, and they were taking him to the hospital.

I had a really sick feeling that it was bad.

On the trip to the hospital, I told Michael he was gone. I knew it. I couldn't stop sobbing. He kept saying, "Stop, we know nothing. He could be fine."

When we arrived at the hospital, there were two uniformed cops outside that had been on the scene. They did not know much but said that the man they brought in was listed as John Doe, age thirty-five. (Dad didn't have his wallet on him.) I thought, *Oh,*

Dad would have loved that age—only thirty-five. He was forty-nine but really didn't look it at all.

Inside the ER, we met Mom and Andrea, They kept us waiting a bit, and then a nurse came out and asked us if we recognized a bracelet that he had been wearing. It was his one and only gold herring bone bracelet, and for some reason, I thought that was a good sign.

They directed us to a back room, where the doctor said the words no on ever wants to hear about anyone they love: "I'm sorry. There was nothing we could do." Shock and pain hit me like a tidal wave. My father was killed in a fatal car accident, and my whole world crumbled. I was fractured, split in half. My heart was shattered into too many pieces to pick up. *How could this be?* My father, my rock, the love of my life was gone, taken from me at only age forty-nine.

I could not breathe.

We all stared at each other. I regret not going into the room to see him one last time. Today I would have, but at that moment I could not bring myself.

There was no other choice but to get in the car and drive home without him. It was a long, painful drive, and it was also the first time we all put our seatbelts on. It was not a habit we had in 1986, but from that day on, I never drove without mine. When we got back to the house it all became very real. The tears flowed and have not stopped to this day.

Family and friends started showing up at my parents' small cond. Everyone was shocked, saddened, and horrified beyond belief.

My aunts came and held me while I cried. *How could this strong, healthy beautiful man we all love so much be gone without a warning or a good-bye?* I started looking at life differently that day. I realized how quickly a life can change, how quickly you can lose someone, and just how fragile life is.

The next few days were a blur. There were funeral arrangements and everything that goes along with handling a loved one's death. Michael was there and took care of most of it, thank God. He was there to run the show because my mom, Andrea and I were grief-stricken, in shock, and barely functioning. It was Halloween a few days later, and the doorbell kept ringing with kids looking for treats, but our door was not opening for any of them. We remained behind closed doors in shock and sorrow.

I got through the funeral with a little help from some Valium that Michael fed me every now and again. I would later take sleeping pills because my sleep was fitful, and I would wake up crying, hoping it was all a mistake. I was missing my father more than anyone could imagine. I could not comprehend how my life could go on with out him in it. He was had always been and still way my whole world. Michael bought me a dog to ease my pain and take my mind off my grief. Ruffles, my beautiful, buff cocker spaniel stayed with me for the next fourteen years and two more addresses.

My very first therapist was Laura. When I hired her, I was twenty-four, married one year, and still in deep dark grief over the sudden loss of my dad. I remember exactly where I was: pacing around the upstairs of our first home, talking to her on the phone. I had called her a few days earlier and was so happy to have her return my call. I was referred to her name by my Aunt Lucia. I had been going to her for advice. She told me she thought I needed help—more help that she could give me, especially because we were talking about her sister, and it was too close. I never thought about therapy in my life, but I knew I needed help. So I took the phone number and called right away.

As I paced in my home that day, Laura told me she was too busy and was not taking on any new clients. She suggested a 12-step program called Adult Children of Alcoholics. I begged. I told her I was at the end of my rope. I had been going to Ala-teen and Ala-non my entire life. She must have heard the desperation in my voice, and I'm sure there was some divine intervention involved. She gave me an appointment on the following Tuesday night at nine o'clock. I showed up. I was a total mess. Grief ridden, desperate and lost.

Her office was actually a large closet in an old home that had been converted to offices. We sat there, and we smoked and talked and smoked some more. It was 1986, back when it was still acceptable to smoke just about anywhere. You could even still smoke in hospital rooms. I poured out my heart. But I was scared of the vulnerability, so I canceled a lot.

It was not easy opening up and being vulnerable, feeling those horrible feelings. But I kept going back, and Laura never gave up on me. She counseled me; she helped me process my grief. I cried an ocean of tears in that little office. She helped me dig deep into my soul.

Laura taught me about codependency and the role it played in my life. She gave me Melody Beattie's first book, *Codependent No More*. It had just come out that year, and I devoured it. I met myself on every page. Melody Beattie was speaking my language. And just a little bit of my life started to make sense.

I started to understand the codependent patterns I had with my mother. If you look up *codependency* in the dictionary, this is what it says: "excessive emotional or psychological reliance on a partner or family member, typically one who requires support due to an illness or addiction" or "a psychological condition or a relationship in which a person is controlled or manipulated by another who is affected with a pathological condition" (such as an addiction to alcohol or drugs). I was there in the definition. I had allowed it to happen for so many years but had not been aware of what was really going on. I thought anyone would worry about a mother that was addicted to pain pills and alcohol. My worry was beyond a normal worry it became an obsession.

It was slowly sinking in, and I was just beginning to unravel the web I had been in since I was a child.

Around that time, my mother continued to be out of control with her alcohol and drug abuse, so I had plenty of time to practice not being codependent. When she was sober, she picked up a new hobby of making cheesecakes. She made them for everybody and every celebration. People requested her cheesecakes and even paid her for them. This kept her busy, at least, and off the streets. Her cheesecake recipe was extraordinary.

Soon after my dad died, I decided I really wanted a baby, and I was sure it would be a boy. I got pregnant quickly; by January of the following year, I was pregnant with little Michael, just three months after my dad died. I focused my attention on my pregnancy, read all the books, and continued working at the DAs office until I was eight months pregnant and had awful sciatica and decided to resign. There was no question that I would be a stay-at-home mom and enjoy every moment of raising my son. I was still in therapy with Laura, and she was one of the first people I called when I learned I was pregnant.

The labor was long—twenty-two hours—and of course painful. But when the baby finally arrived on an autumn day in 1987 at 7:14 p.m., weighing in at 7 lbs. 4 oz., I could not have been more joyful. As I had suspected, it was a boy. And the joy just spread into my heart the minute I looked at him. Even though he had the pointiest head from being in the birth canal for over an hour and was born with clubfeet, I didn't care. I loved him more than I thought was humanly possible.

Once he arrived and I was back in my room, I had a feeling of empowerment. It felt like I had arrived. I could do anything, and I was invincible. I think a little bit of that feeling is with me still. I had this little boy to love, and joy started to replace the pain and sorrow.

Little Michael brought us so much happiness and hope, and he continues to. He was so much fun while he was growing up. We spent all our days and nights together, and I loved every minute of it—not so much the 2 a.m. feedings and sleep deprivation, but that goes with the territory. I was so fortunate because it was not long before he was sleeping through the night. And I mean *sleeping* twelve hours and sometimes even fourteen. I always checked on him to make sure he was still breathing and would jump to meet him the minute he woke up.

It took a very long time to get over my dad's death. But little by little, Laura helped me feel better and find peace. I would miss my dad always, but now my son was healing my heart.

My husband eventually decided that he wanted to move upstate, New York, to open a pizzeria with his cousin. I was dead against it, but I felt like I had no choice. I thought that if I did not let him pursue his dreams, he would ultimately resent me. I didn't realize that I would end up resenting him for never listening or giving any credence to what I said, felt, or desire. It was his way—the Bible according to Michael.

I was so upset. I was finally living in my beloved town where all of my friends lived, and I had to leave. What a cruel joke. We lived on Dally Road for only two years before we left. I didn't want to go at all, but I did.

I started seriously questioning my marriage. I believed I loved my husband, but what did I know about love? I didn't even know who I was when we met. I was lost and confused. He brought me comfort; I saw him as shelter from the shit storm of my life. I probably needed the control and the structure where there never had been any before. I quickly realized that it wasn't how I wanted to live the rest of my life.

I didn't want to move for so many reasons. My mom was really sick at the time and would die within the next two years. I had loved my little house in the neighborhood of my dreams so much. I didn't want to leave my friends and family.

Little Michael was eight months old when we moved. And it was the beginning of the end of my marriage. I would stay in it another eight years, but it was over the day the moving truck pulled up to my cute little house and drove off with all of our things.

Michael didn't even wait for me or let me follow him upstate to our new home. He took off with the moving van and just said, "You know where you're going." But I didn't. So I packed little Michael in the car, and with my sister-in-law Bee driving behind me, off we went. My dad had been dead only about a year. I was leaving my little dream home. My mom was dying, my sister was lost, and I had a hole in my heart like nobody knew.

Chapter 10

A Love Letter to My Father

Dear Daddy,

I miss you. I never got to say good-bye to the love of my life, my dad.

At age forty-nine, just two months before your fiftieth birthday, you left me. I'm not sure if you meant to go or if you wanted to go, but you did. You were taken away in a swift moment on a corner in Staten Island while pulling onto our street. You were the best driver. I don't know how that happened.

I hope you know how much I loved you and continue to love you to this day. I look for signs that you are still around me. You were always there for me, no matter what anyone else says. I knew I could always depend on you. You were only a phone call away. You did your best with being a parent. I truly believe you did the best you could with what you knew. I know this for sure.

Your dad died when you were a baby, and your life was never easy growing up. I'm not sure what kind of a mom your mom was to you, but I always knew you loved me. I was Daddy's little girl. You made me feel special and pretty and protected and worthy. You were the Man of Steel, remember? My own personal Superman. The first time I saw you bleed, I was truly shocked that your blood was red and not blue.

So please know how much I loved you and love you to this day. I will continue loving you until we meet again. I will miss you as long as I walk this earth. I will miss your laugh, your walk, your voice, your scent, your kindness, and your love always.

When I think of you, I think about a man who loved his family, worked hard, and tried his best to make his way in this crazy world. A man who was always eager and ready to lend a helping hand. I will remember your kindness. And what else is more important in life than loving-kindness? You taught me that. I am who I am today because of you.

It's been thirty years since I've kissed your cheek or embraced you. But I will never forget the feelings, the love, the warmth, and the comfort of the most amazing dad any girl could hope for.

My Superman, my Joe Cool, my love, my dad, my heart.

Love, Your end of the rainbow, your pot of gold, me

Chapter 11

Lost Road, Upstate New York

When I arrived at Lost Road that day with little Michael, the movers were already moving us into our new home in the middle of nowhere. It felt like a dream—and not a dream I had ever wished for or imagined. I was not a country girl.

I remember going down to the basement and being introduced to a new variety of insect I had never known, the earwig. The place was infested. Then I was told why this little ugly creature got its name: because they crawl inside a person's ear and fester there. *Please, somebody help me. Get me out of here. Bring me back to civilization.*

Living in the middle of nowhere with Michael was simply not a good idea. I did not fit in. I did not blend. I did not like it there. I was a city girl. I had lived in Brooklyn and Staten Island my whole life, and I had worked and played in New York City. At the time, I loved fashion. It was the eighties, but I was living in the sticks. They didn't even pick up your garbage or deliver your mail. There was no place to shop! WTF?

I never felt so alone as I did during that time. I had felt lonely many times in my life, but this was a whole new level. I had my first anxiety attack there.

Even after I moved and was no longer in treatment with Laura, she continued to guide and support me. She became my friend and surrogate mother, and I love her more than she could ever know. I always said that God may have given me a screwed-up family life, but he gave me the most amazing therapists to work it all out. Laura was the first and showed me what a great therapist can be. The bar was high, and I found a few others that brought me peace over the next thirty years—all angels who helped me see and feel my way through the layers of one really crazy, fucked up onion.

Life in upstate was quiet—very different from anything I had ever experienced. It turned out that the pizzeria was not going to be in our town. It opened an hour or so away, It was successful, and for two years, that's what my husband did. He left at ten in the morning and commuted an hour to work, sometimes with the only car we had. He came home at eleven at night.

I was so lonely that I considered inviting the Jehovah Witness people in for coffee when they rang my bell. The upside was that I got to spend uninterrupted blissful time with my son. It was just little Michael and I. Endless days and nights to bond and have fun. A blessing in disguise for both of us.

I read to him endlessly. He loved his books and was able to recite most of them back to me by the time he started talking. Together, we had tons of fun. We had Ruffles, our beloved cocker spaniel, to play with as well. We watched many a Disney movie. In that respect, I would not trade that time in for anything.

Michael was a curious, bright, and beautiful baby, and he filled my days with much joy and laughter. I loved him like I loved no one else in the world. He kept me going. He filled that hole in my heart that was the loss of my dad. And he filled it in a million countless ways. Would I have been having this experience if I still lived in Staten Island? Yes, but minus the isolation. I would have been sharing it with my girlfriends and their babies. The isolation was getting to me, and I was feeling depressed.

I called Laura a few times, telling her how I was feeling. She told me she had a vacation home in upstate New York, and that she would come up to see me. And she did, many times. She and her husband, Angel, gave me hope and comfort on those visits. She reminded me of who I was and everything I had been working toward. She told me I was not depressed, just a little beaten down and lonely. She also promised and reminded me that my wings were still intact—I just needed to remember how to use them.

Laura gave me tips on what to do with my time, and I took her up on them. I became a classic movie buff, watching the AMC channel when Michael went to sleep at night. I started meditating and got really good at it. I was able to bring myself to a more peaceful place when I needed to. She told me to experiment with makeup when I was bored. (This coming from a woman who did not wear a bit of it herself.) And I did what she said. I took her prescriptions for filling my days, and they worked. I started to feel better. One baby step and lots of long, slow breathing. I slowly began to feel centered and strong.

So in that very lonely dark place, I had begun to find ways to soothe my soul. It was the first steps on my deeper spiritual path. It wasn't a path with the Catholic girl going to church and saying a few prayers. It was when I started to realize I could find strength in something greater than myself. And that was also when I started to meditate with guided meditations on tape and was able to hold space for myself and connect with my breath and heart.

I became pregnant with my daughter Angelica and wanted to have a less stressful pregnancy, so I stepped into my life and didn't focus as much on my mother. I got a frown or two from my aunts, but they didn't know what I had been going through my whole life with their sister. They thought they did, but they did not.

I recently had a conversation with my aunt Peggy, and she told me that one of the scariest moments in her life was the one time she saw my mother have a seizure. She was terrified by it. So, I said, "Can you imagine being the child that saw that all the time and feared the next time? Can you imagine the horror of thinking your mother is dead in front of you?" She said she could not.

Chapter 12

My Mother's Death and Burial

My mom died when I was living upstate. One of the most tragic, earth-shattering, saddest days of my life, other than the day my father was killed, was the day I buried my mother.

She had been sick most of my life, but after my dad died, she went downhill fast. My father had taken out a life insurance policy. He listed the beneficiaries as my sister, my mom, and me, with everything to be split three ways. He also had a very large pension that was also to be split three ways. After he died, my mother convinced my sister and me that it was wrong for us to take our share. She needed to live the rest of her life, and she felt it was best if we signed the money over to her. So we did—fools that we were.

My mother then proceeded to spend that money any way she could for the next three years before she died. She became a big fan of TV shopping shows and bought whatever she wanted. Hundreds of thousands of dollars were spent, down to a pittance that she left to her sisters. The remaining money went to my son and my unborn child, Angelica, whom I was five months pregnant with.

The Darvon and alcohol abuse continued and was wreaking havoc on her body, especially her intestines. They were not working well, and they were sluggish. The Darvon was not allowing them to function properly. She would get a blockage in her intestines and would be vomiting bile for days until she had to be hospitalized.

The procedure was to stick a tube into her nose and down her throat to suck the bile out. It was disgusting. If the blockage couldn't resolve itself, it was back to the operating table for more surgery, which would result in more adhesions and more blockages. It was a vicious cycle.

In the last year of her life, she could not eat solid food. She was hooked up to a machine that fed her some kind of milky white liquid through a port. Not being able to eat is not really living. She was in and out the hospital quite a bit during the last two years of her life. But then again, she was in and our some type of hospital most of my life. She was getting sicker by the day.

Then one morning in August, while I was staying in Staten Island, I called her hospital room to see how she was, and a nurse answered and said she was having a seizure, and they were working on her. By the time I got to hospital, within thirty minutes or less, she was in a coma, which she remained in for five days. She was asleep for her fiftieth birthday and dead three days later on a sad August day. My mother was finally gone. No more suffering.

My mother's burial was an extremely traumatic day for my family. Out of everything that I went through in my life, it was one of the hardest days because I loved my family. It was a day of sadness, confusion, abandonment, and violence. A day it took me years to even remotely wrap my head around. I had to stay strong because I was five months pregnant. I held it together somewhat until my daughter was born and then the melt downs took place.

I ended up having to be on an anti-depressant for 5 months so I could function and back into therapy for a few more years.

I don't have many pictures of my mother in my house. I don't quote her like some of my girlfriends quote their moms. It's too painful to remember everything. I was always afraid to discuss my childhood and my mother with anyone for fear that they would judge me and think I was a terrible person. Perhaps putting this out there now will cause some to judge me, but that's okay.

It's incredibly difficult to imagine what I went through if you didn't have a similar childhood. So I have compassion for those who don't understand, even for my own family members, whom I love dearly. And I know for every person who doesn't understand or relate, there has to be a person who does. If my story resonates with, helps, heals, or comforts just one person in some way, I have accomplished my mission in revealing my truth and sharing my message.

When I gave birth to my sweet Angelica, I remember wondering, *How will I know how to mother my daughter?* It was a big question, one of many. We don't get a handbook. But I can tell you this: I did well. I raised a strong, kind, compassionate, and beautiful girl whom I admire, treasure and adore. She's my best friend for life, my shopping, cooking, and beach buddy. I know I am far from perfect and made my share of mistakes but for the most part I raised her well.

I never laugh harder than I do with my children, but especially with Angelica. She laughs until she cries, and it's infectious. I have a son that any mother would be proud of—a boy I have watched grow up to be a strong, kind, compassionate, and good human being. I think, *I did it. I did that.* It's a miracle in itself, and I am so proud of both of my children.

After my mother died, I really wanted to move back to Staten Island. I told Michael I had had enough of the country life and said I was plotting a way to get out of there. I also said that if he didn't put a For Sale sign on the front lawn, he'd find me gone one night when he got home from the pizzeria. So we put the house up for sale, but we did not move back to Staten Island as I wished. We "compromised" and moved to little more down state, a little closer to home which would always be Staten Island and civilization.

It all turned out to be a blessing. Fate had intervened, because as the story goes, I would not have met my future husband, Liam, if we hadn't moved to our next address.

Chapter 13

The Unraveling Somewhat Down State, New York

I was singing at the top of my lungs in the moving van as we pulled out of the driveway of Lost Road. I can't remember the name of the song I was singing, but I was belting it out and feeling very joyful. I was getting out of the sticks. And though I wasn't going exactly where I thought I wanted to be, anything was better than where I had been in the middle of nowhere. Our new home was only a forty five minute drive to Staten Island. I was getting closer to civilization and home at least.

We decided on new construction, which was exciting. I had never lived in a brand-new home as an adult. It was fun picking out everything and witnessing the process as our home was being built. Since my parents' deaths, Andrea had lived with me here and there. She had lived with us for while in every house we lived in since my parents deaths. Switching back and forth from our home and the home of her best friend, Brianna, whose mother loved Andrea like one of her own. I will always be eternally grateful to her family for the love and support they show us. Andrea and Brianna met in the fourth grade, and like my girlfriends and me, remained friends for life. I love Brianna like a sister, too.

Michael and I decided to build an apartment in the basement for Andrea in our new home. That way, she could have a place of her own, and we could all have our privacy. I forfeited buying dining-room furniture so we could build her apartment. But about six months after it was completed, she got back together with her boyfriend, Phil, who would later become her husband. So there we were with a lovely apartment and no one to inhabit it. We never rented it and instead used it for guests and parties. It turned out to be a really good thing.

When we moved in, Michael was three and Angelica was eight months old. The housing development was fairly new with lots of young children—the perfect place to raise a family. It was there, too, that I found my second tribe. It didn't happen right away, but little by little, it started to develop.

First I met my friend Valentina through the preschool that my son and her daughter attended. Next came Nancy who did Valentina 's nails, and I soon became a client and a friend. Then, while the kids were in CCD, I met Doreen, Eva, and Patti. We were the original crew. We called ourselves the Six-Pack, though beer was not our thing. We liked our wine for sure! Back then it was White Zinfandel right out of the box. We were thick as thieves and always there for each other. Eva's son, Joseph, and my son Michael met in the second grade and are still best friends.

My in-laws stayed with us quite a bit. They would come upstate every few weekends or so from Staten Island to babysit the kids. By that time, we had opened another pizzeria/restaurant in not far from our home, and I worked there on the weekends when they came up to visit. Later, when we opened a bigger place, I worked most Friday and Saturday nights, tending the bar. I was able to find two lovely babysitters, who would alternate weekends when we needed them. It was a fun and exciting time.

We had a good life for to the naked eye, but our marriage started to crumble. When I look at the years I was married to Michael, it is like looking back at a hurricane. It all happened so fast. There was so much living and dying packed into one decade: our marriage on September 1985; the tragic death of my dad on October, 1986; the blissful birth of our son, on September 1987; the dramatic move from Staten Island to Upstate, New York (a.k.a. The Middle of Nowhere); the death of my mom on August, 1989; the loss of my entire family over money, in 1989; the birth of my beautiful daughter, in the winter of 1989; and another move from Lost Road to being found again in August of 1992. There was no time to catch our breath, come up for air, or have a moment of clarity.

Finally, from 1992 to 1995, I felt very alone. I started seeing very clearly that my marriage was a one-way street, and it was not actually a relationship. I had no say in most matters. I thought I did, but I did not. Whatever I said was not taken into consideration. It was Michael's way or no way—or at least that was my perception. I was being controlled in a way that took me almost ten years to figure out. But I realize now that I did need some control or structure, and he provided that for that part of my life. If the years I spent with Michael were a hurricane, the years before I met him were a tsunami.

We argued like most couples about family or money. I didn't handle the money and didn't have a clue about our finances. It became clear to me during those years in the early 1990s that we were not doing well financially. The restaurant was not doing well, and we didn't have any savings. We lived a comfortable life, but we were living above our means. *Way* above.

I was very unhappy in my marriage, feeling like a bystander. I told Michael many times that I was unhappy and that things needed to change. Over the years I made many requests for change but they fell on deaf ears.

I thought about divorce constantly, but I could not imagine how I could do it on my own. I had two small children, no money, a high school education, and zero family except my sister, who had her own problems. Where would I go? What would I do? How would I survive?

It seemed impossible, but there was a spark of hope in me, a stirring that said, "You can do this. You deserve to be happy. You matter, and you deserve a better life." I remember crying to Laura on the phone. I was so afraid to get divorced; I pictured myself living in a box or in a rusty car somewhere. I felt like I had nothing, and I especially felt like I had no one. I didn't want to be alone, and I didn't want to hurt the father of my children. He was a man who tried his best to love me and take care of me. Laura said she would rather see me on welfare than see me so unhappy and that she would always be there for me.

Then I thought about my children. *How can I do this to them?* I wanted them to have the life I did not. I thought about Michael moving on. *Then who will he meet? How will another woman enter my precious babies' lives? How will they be treated?* I think that scared me the most. I was so, so scared, but that little glimmer of hope would sometimes rise above my fears and whisper in my ear that it was going to be okay. I prayed for guidance, I wrote in my journal, and I cried an ocean of tears.

I finally mustered up the courage and asked for a divorce in September of 1995. I could not celebrate another anniversary. I could not smile through it and act as if everything was okay, because it wasn't. He was shocked and tried everything he could to sway my decision, but it was too late for that.

I had built up walls of resentment over the years, and they could not be penetrated. I had fallen out of love, and I could not get it back. I didn't want to be divorced, but I didn't see myself staying with a man I wasn't in love with and felt deeply unhappy with. Even though divorcing would make my life a mess again in a major way, I had to do it. I had to try. I cared about Michael, and he knew he always had a place in my heart, but I had to do what was best for the children and me. I deserved to be happy, and I knew I was worthy of true love. I didn't want my children to think it's okay to stay in an unhappy, phony or love-less marriage. I needed real. I deserved real. I could feel it in my future.

It was a struggle and a very tumultuous two years before the divorce was final, and it cost me so much money that I did not have. The stress was unbearable. I was going to have to pay the lawyer when I sold the house. It was a sad and anxiety-filled time. I was terrified about not having any money. I could not afford a thing except for food and whatever my children needed, and of course, the mortgage and any other bills I had. I didn't buy myself a thing, and I was barely making ends meet. But I felt a sense of peace. A peace I had not felt before. Michael was very kind and went above and beyond to help me with the kids. He was always there for them, never missing a weekend or even a poetry reading.

—

I held onto my faith in God and in the Blessed Mother. I prayed and prayed and wrote in my journal long into the night.

I decided to rent out the apartment downstairs, which had remained empty since my sister moved out. I wanted to rent it through word-of-mouth because I had to make sure someone knew the person personally. Although it had a separate entrance, there was still access to my home as well. I wanted to keep the kids in the house as long as I could and not cause more change and upset.

I started asking around through friends and got the word out. The first person to come was a sweet young girl named Kara. She had just graduated from college and was going to be starting her first job in September as a first-grade teacher. She loved the apartment and practically begged to move in. She had been looking at other places, and none was as new and clean as mine. I was thrilled to have her, and we became fast friends.

I was used to cooking for four, so Kara would often come upstairs and have dinner with Michael, Angelica, and me. If she got home late, I would take her dinner down or have it waiting for her at the door. I loved having her in the house. It made me feel a little less lonely, and it was great for her, too. Besides college, it was her first time on her own, so it worked out well for both of us. She would babysit sometimes and help the kids with math homework. I can't do math to save myself, so this was a blessing.

Kara had a boyfriend at the time, but a year later, they broke up. She started dating a guy named Matt, whom she met at a club in, New Jersey. She told me about her adventures with Matt and going on endless rides on the back of his Harley. She was in love and having so much fun—and I was living vicariously through her. She would now and again mention one of Matt's friends, Liam, whom they would go riding with and hang out with.

During the first couple of years of my divorce, I dated two guys briefly. I was alone most of the time when the kids went to see their dad every other weekend and for two weeks in the summer. I was not interested in the bar scene at all, and my friends were married with families. I felt like a fish out of water. I remember going to the mall alone and seeing families together, with Mom, Dad, and children, and feeling very sad, lonely, and isolated.

Over the next couple of years, Kara continued to talk to me about Liam, Matt's friend. She would come home from a weekend with Matt in New Jersey and say how much she wanted me to meet him. She would go on about how cute he was, how nice he was, and funny, too. He was dating someone, then was engaged to another one, and then was kind of living with someone else. I told her he sounded great, and if he were ever single for a minute to please let me know. We laughed, and time moved on.

Then one day, Kara in the spring of 1999, said she had run into Liam having pizza at a local bar. He was having dinner by himself, and he joined her and Matt. She asked him about his current girlfriend, and he replied that they had broken up. With that, Liam said to Kara, "You're a nice girl, Kara. You must have nice girlfriends."

Kara said of course and could not wait to tell him all about me. She started out by saying that she was not sure how he would feel dating a divorced woman with two small children.

He replied, "I'll give it a shot," and the rest, as they say, is history.

We decided to go out on a blind date, sight unseen and never having even spoken on the phone. It was a weekend that I didn't have the kids, and it was decided that I would drive down to Jersey and meet them at bar/restaurant for dinner and drinks. Kara generally spent the weekends with Matt in New Jersey, so I agreed to take the drive.

However, on the way down, I started to panic and question why I was driving so far to meet this guy and why they hadn't come up to see me. With much trepidation, I parked my car, checked my lipstick in the rearview mirror, tied the belt to my leather jacket a little tighter, and went into the restaurant. They were sitting in the back at the bar, and the walk from the front door to meet them seemed like an eternity with all eyes on me. (Maybe I was being a little paranoid.) They ordered me a glass of wine, and the night took off.

When I first laid eyes on Liam, I thought, *He's not my type. I date shorter, darker, Italian guys.* Then I thought, *Well, that never really worked out, did it?* He was very cute and funny. I laughed so much that night. He and Matt fed off each other, and they were like a comedy act. So we had a great night, and when it was time to say good-bye, I did not want the night to end.

Liam walked me to my car and said that he was going to give me the number to his hotline and that I should call him anytime. I retorted, "Well, here's my number. I am very available anytime," which kind of came out wrong. What I meant was that I was practically a stay-at-home mom and could be reached anytime. I told him that if he wanted to see me again, he could and should call *me.* He mentioned something about me playing like a girl or doing the girl thing, and I said yes. Off he went. No good-night kiss or any promises.

The phone number I gave him was my house number. I'm not even sure if I had a cell phone then. That first date was on a Saturday night in April of 1999, and I was anxiously hoping to hear from him again soon.

I guess you could say I was smitten for sure. There was a warmth in his eyes that reminded me of my dad's. It doesn't get any better than that in my book. So I continued with my weekend, waiting patiently and wondering when or if he would call me.

Kara and I had a Monday-night ritual. I would put the kids to bed, she would come upstairs a little before nine, and we would watch *Ally McBeal*, polish our nails, and have a glass of red wine. It was the perfect Monday night as far as we were concerned. Well, it got even better when around 9:15, when my house phone rang and the caller ID showed it was Liam with a New Jersey number. *Oh my God! It's him, it's him! Okay, calm down. Catch your breath.* I answered the phone very calmly, as if I had no idea who was on the other end. "Hello?"

He sounded happy to hear my voice. We talked about the date and what a great time we'd had. Then he asked me out for the following Saturday. I said no because I had the kids but told him I would love to see him the next weekend. I do not know how it happened, but he persuaded me to get a sitter and come out. So I did.

The following weekend, Liam really wanted to take me to his favorite restaurant in New Jersey, a little French cafe. He wanted us to have a really nice meal together in one of his favorite spots. It was the first of many, many meals in this romantic cafe, which promptly became my favorite restaurant. I would come to know the whole cast of characters very well. Liam had met the owner and chef years before, when they were working at the same club/ restaurant together. Liam was a door host, a term I'd never heard of in my life; in New York, we called them bouncers. Kenny was cooking, and Matt, Kara's boyfriend, was the bartender. In that same club, Kara had met Matt years later.

That was it—we never stopped dating. I would see Liam every other weekend at first, and he would come up on Wednesdays for dinner. I had to come with some more eclectic menu options. Since I was a single parent on a tight budget, I was making pasta fagioli a couple of times a week. Chicken cutlet with canned corn and salad was the other staple. I thought I would wow him with my homemade sauce, meatballs, and braciola.

I really took my time with stuffing the braciola using fresh parsley and garlic and the best Parmesan I could find. I added these ingredients to my meatballs as well. Well, as it turned out, he did not eat garlic or Parmesan cheese, so that one backfired. I used those two ingredients in all of my cooking, so something would have to give. Today, Liam eats garlic, can handle sliced Parmesan reggiano, but still no grated cheese for this man.

Eventually, he visited on the weekends I had the kids, too. I always set him up in the guest room if he was staying over. I made sure to keep things very legitimate for the children, and we continued that policy until the day we got married. We were both old-fashioned in that way, and I wouldn't change the arrangement at all. I had to keep Michael and Angelica's well-being in mind first and always. It was hard enough for them to come to terms with mom having a boyfriend. I wanted to teach them the right values and morals as well.

Liam was an arborist who still owns his own tree service to this day, and he is very much into plants and landscaping. His house was always beautifully landscaped, and he planted tons of flowers each spring. I was not in a position to spend money on plants at that time, and I was happy with whatever was popping up from the year before. I taught CCD on Wednesdays. I really enjoyed teaching the class, and it meant that Michael and Angelica could attend free.

One Wednesday, as I was arriving home with the kids, there was Liam with a truck full of mulch and flats and flats of beautiful begonias and marigolds. He was landscaping the front of my house, and I was very happy and surprised. He said he wanted me to have a smile on my face every time I drove into the driveway. This is just one of the many surprises, smiles and absolute magic he has brought into my life.

I had known Liam only a month or two when he asked me to take a trip with him to Hawaii. He never had been to Hawaii and actually never took vacations, being a proclaimed workaholic. My friends all thought I was crazy to say yes because we had just met. But I knew in my heart it would be fine. So he booked a trip for us to go to Maui and stay at the Four Seasons for my birthday in July.

First, he wanted to take me to Lake Placid, New York. He had gone to forestry school a few towns away and always passed a beautiful hotel on the lake. He had wanted to go but told me he never wanted to take anyone there until me. I was thrilled.

We picked a weekend that the kids were with their dad, and we drove up north on a perfectly beautiful, sunny day in June in Liam's green convertible Corvette. The views were gorgeous. I had never been to Lake Placid, and we were both excited to be taking the trip together.

Liam entertained me with stories about the many times he took the ride while going back and forth to college and how he drove up the very first time with his right arm in a sling after having surgery. We marveled that his parents let him do that—drive 280 miles with one arm in a snowstorm. He pointed out different mountains and waterfalls and, of course, the different trees.

The hotel was beautiful and majestic. We walked in the front doors, where there was a beautiful grand stairway, and everything was covered in custom woodwork. The fireplaces were going, even though it was June, and we were greeted by a very friendly staff and shown to our beautiful room.

It was that weekend and in that room that Liam and I knew we were in love for sure. We said our first I-love-yous and were like two little kids amazed that we had found each other. It was a perfect weekend, and I had not felt that giddy in years. Not to say that I was totally unhappy before I met Liam, but this took happy to another level.

The trip to Maui was approaching, and I had nothing to wear. I had stopped buying myself new clothes a few years earlier, when I got divorced, because I needed every last dime for the kids' needs, food, and bills. Kara came to the rescue with a bunch of summer dresses. Luckily, we were the same size. And my friend Carole across the street loaned me some cover-ups, sarongs, and other accessories. I was ready for the trip!

I packed my bag and drove to Liam's for the evening so we could get up early together and head to the airport. As was customary,

I met Michael at a Dunkin' Donuts right near the exit from Liam's to transfer the kids to him for the week I would be away. I hated leaving them, but they were scheduled for two weeks each summer with him, and this was one of them. It happened to fall on the same week they vacationed with Michael's whole family at a resort in the Catskills, so they were okay with me leaving.

We arrived in Maui, and the hotel and our room blew me away. I was the most beautiful hotel in Maui. It was spectacular with its open-air lobby and bars. The restaurants were amazing, and the staff practically tied our shoes.

One of the most surreal moments for me was when I was sitting at the pool one day wanting to pinch myself. I was next to Liam, feeling so blessed for the love that we shared, and sipping on a frosty cocktail. I had my eyes closed, and although I was safe and happy, I still had that little voice in the back of my head saying, *Who do you think you are? How are you even going to pay your bills this month?* Then I heard a voice say, "Chilled towel, Miss?"

I opened my eyes, and standing before me was an adorable young Hawaiian man holding a silver tray and tongs with a chilled towel for me to cool off with. I took his towel with a polite thank-you, and then he asked if I wanted a spritz. *Sure!* And he spritzed me down with a bottle of Evian water spray, refilled my water glass with more Evian, and was on his way. I relaxed, took another sip of my drink, and thought, *Fuck the bills. I'm staying in this glorious, somewhat unreal moment, and I hope it never ends.*

After that, Liam asked us to take a trip to Maine with him. His friend Timmy had a cabin on a lake, and although it was mostly a man cave, it was a very special place to him, and he wanted us to go. Liam and his friends had been traveling up to the cabin in Maine since 1980. They would all pile into their cars, usually right after a night working at the club, and make their annual pilgrimage to the cabin. At that time I might have been one of the first girlfriends of any of the guys to venture up there. I think Timmy's then-girlfriend and now wife might have been, and she warned me about big ants and spiders the size of small crabs. She was not lying, but the beauty of the lake and Maine itself was worth it all.

That was the first of many trips to Maine and of many fond memories. There was no cell phone reception at the time and no TV, so we got to spend fun, quality time together. The lake was so beautiful, and the sunsets were magic. We would take the kids out on the water all day long. We would find the perfect spot, throw the anchor down, and have a picnic lunch on the boat. Then Liam and the kids would snorkel, and I would get to kick back and catch some sun. We would take the boat into town and go to the our favorite restaurant which is known for its famous duck dinners.

The cabin was tiny and always smelled a little musty, so we stocked up on air fresheners and candles. It didn't really matter because we spent almost every waking hour outside, either on the boat or eating at the picnic table or around the campfire at night. This was a family favorite as it involved s'mores, and we loved to make them as much as we loved to eat them. The kids would go in search of the perfect stick, and we'd work on the art of the perfectly browned marshmallow. The ones that burned got thrown in the fire. The ingredients always had to be Nabisco Graham Cracker with Hershey milk chocolate squares, and of course, the perfectly browned Kraft marshmallows. The joy of squishing the Peggy, chocolate, and warm, creamy marshmallow together and taking that first delicious bite was heavenly.

Calories did not count while staying at the cabin in Maine; we ate countless s'mores and lobster dripping in butter, and we drank gin and tonics in red plastic solo cups. Aside from being able to spend wonderful days and night with my children and Liam, I also loved how relaxed Liam was when we were there.

Our travels with the children continued. That winter we took the kids up to the Adirondaks for the Goodwill Games. Every hotel was booked except for one very expensive lodge. Children under twelve were not allowed, and they only had one room left, which was a two-level suite called the Birds Eye View. We booked it and told the kids they were twelve and thirteen.

It was a magical time. It snowed and snowed the entire time we were there, and we got to go cross-country skiing on the golf course in the most magnificent, soft snow. It was a day I will never forget. There was hardly anyone else on the slopes, and it was an ethereal atmosphere. Little did I ever imagine that Liam and I would be getting married in that beautiful place in just a few years.

The lodge was set up as a retreat for unwinding and unplugging. They didn't even have TVs in the rooms. Liam and I wanted to go to the darling little pub downstairs for a drink, but the kids were restless. He somehow talked the management into finding a TV and hooking it up in our suite. I don't know whom he paid or how he did it, but they were content, and we got to go out.

We sat at the bar in a dreamy little pub while the snow fell outside, and I wanted to pinch myself, I was so happy. I ordered a B&B to drink, and we had a delicious gooey dessert. It was heaven. I felt as light as the snowflakes falling outside as I sat with Liam as the fireplace roared and my heart hummed.

Not very long after I met Liam, Kara decided to move in with Matt in New Jersey. They settled into a cute apartment in New Jersey, just a few streets away from Liam's house. I missed her so much and hated to see her go, but I was happy for her. The other problem was that her rent paid the other half of my mortgage.

Liam and I discussed how to make things work out so that Michael, Angelica, and I could stay in the house. The thought of renting to someone else was not appealing, and I was barely making ends meet as it was. We decided it was best for me to sell the house.

I spoke to Michael, and we began the process. It was sad to leave the home we had lived in for ten years and where I had watched my babies grow up, but it was time. I took one more walk through the empty rooms before I left, gathered all my memories, shed a few tears, and off we all went to our little condo on Marks Place.

Journal Excerpt, January 3, 2000

Looking back over this journal and reading it aloud to another human being has been, to say the least, enlightening. I have come so very far. I have grown, I have conquered, and I am still here to tell about it. I will never wonder again if I am strong. How can I possibly question myself? I have the strength of many women with many years of survival. I feel better about myself today than I have ever felt in my life.

I have finally come out of that dark, haunted, lonely abyss into the light of the life I was meant to live: a life of happiness, joy, and laughter. I have never laughed so much in my life than I have in the past six months. I like to laugh. I always wondered what everyone else was laughing about. What was so funny in this crazy, shitty life? When I used to laugh, I did not feel the joy. Now I do. I laugh with a feeling of joy in my heart I never knew before. I cry happy soulful tears of utter freedom. Freedom to just be me. No longer feeling controlled by anything or anyone.

Now I am not afraid, I am not controlled, and I feel lightness in my being. I never thought I would get to this place, but here I am. All the pain and the sorrow the years of getting here were worth it because they make this victory so much sweeter. I can truly enjoy and relish my life because now that I realize the journey I am on is my journey, and it has made me who I am today, and I'm a really good person. I know my journey has and will help me help other people because of the wisdom I have acquired over all these crazy years. I have so much to be grateful for. I have the most amazing and healthy two children any mother could ever pray for, a relationship I have only dreamed of, and friends that are there for me and love me.

I know love, trust, and happiness on a much deeper level. Now I can be the mother, girlfriend, and simply the woman I came here to be—who God intended me to be. Thank you, God, for all the blessings in my life, for never giving up on me and loving me through it all.

Part Three

"Our deepest fear is not that we are inadequate. Our deepest fear is that we are powerful beyond measure. It is our light, not our darkness that most frightens us." Marianne Williamson. *A Return to Love: Reflections on the Principles of "A Course inMiracles"*

Christmas Eve Zuppe Di Pesce

Ingredients:

    3 3-pound lobsters
    4 dozen Little Neck clams
    1 pound large shrimp
    2 dozen mussels
    2 pound calamari
    1/4 cup olive oil
    3 28-ounce cans of crushed tomato
    6 cloves garlic, minced
    5 tablespoons fresh basil, chopped
    3 tablespoons fresh parsley, chopped
    1/4 crushed red pepper flakes
    1/2 teaspoon oregano, dried
    2 pounds linguini

Directions:

Sauté garlic in olive oil until lightly golden. Add tomatoes and cook for 10 minutes until sauce is hot. Keep heat medium low. Add clams and mussels, and cook covered for 5 minutes or until some of the clams begin to open. Add lobster and calamari, and cook 10 minutes. Add shrimp, and cook 5 minutes. Add parsley and basil. Stir, cook an additional 5 minutes, and serve over cooked linguini.

Be-Well-Nourished Quinoa Stuffed Peppers

Ingredients:

 1 medium onion, finely chopped (1 cup)
 2 tablespoons olive oil
 2 large carrots, grated
 2 cloves garlic, minced
 1 cup fresh or frozen peas
 1/2 cup sundried tomatoes chopped
 2 large basil leaves, chopped
 1 cup quinoa
 1/2 cup vegetable stock
 1 15-ounce can diced tomatoes
 2 handfuls of spinach, chopped
 4 large red bell peppers, halved lengthwise, ribs removed
 Sea salt and pepper to taste

Directions:

Heat oil in saucepan over medium heat. Add onion, and cook 5 minutes, or until soft. Add garlic and carrot, sauté 3 minutes. Mix in peas and sundried tomatoes, basil and spinach, and vegetable stock. Cook 5 minutes.

Place 1 cup dry quinoa with 2 cups of water in a medium saucepan. Bring to a boil, reduce heat to simmer, and cover tightly until all water is absorbed. Do not stir. Fluff with fork, and let cool. Gently fold vegetable mixture with cooled quinoa.

Preheat oven to 350 degrees. Pour can of diced tomatoes in bottom of baking dish.

Cut pepper in half, take out seeds, and top with quinoa mixture. Cover with foil, and bake 1 hour. Uncover and cook 30 more minutes or until peppers are starting to brown lightly and are soft to touch. Let stand 5 minutes. Transfer stuffed peppers to serving plates, and drizzle each with tomatoes from pan juices before serving.

Chapter 14

Marks Place, Upstate, New York

It was decided that Liam would buy a condominium, and the kids and I would be his tenants. It was a three-bedroom townhouse in our town so that the kids could remain in their school. I was able to breathe a little bit financially. My monthly bills were much lower, and I didn't have to maintain the property. The kids were not thrilled, but they grew to like it.

I decorated it like a little dollhouse with lots of feminine touches. I was into the country look back then. My friend Doreen came over and stenciled the little kitchen for me in bright- and light-blue stripes. I set up a tiny ice cream parlor table for two in the kitchen. My dining room furniture fit into the small dining space, and that is where we had our meals. We all had our own rooms, and I even had a small master bath. The kids had the hall bath, and there was a small powder room when you walked into the front door. The condo was just the right size for the three of us.

At that time, I had a long-term temporary position as a secretary in the middle school guidance office. I had the same hours and days off as the kids, including snow days and holidays. We drove to and from school together, so it was perfect.

I still gathered girlfriends around my kitchen table every chance I could. That little tribe of women continued to be my best friends and constant support. I don't know what I would have done with out them. I would have them over for birthdays and Christmas parties, and we always had a ton of fun. My life was in a transition again, but I felt safe, loved, and happy. I had to remind myself daily that everything was going to be okay. I was so used to waiting for the other shoe to drop and to living in a state of lack and fear. I had to start flexing my faith muscle and setting positive intentions for myself. I leaned into my faith and stayed focused on my many blessings.

Michael was a freshman in high school, and Angelica was in the sixth grade. I knew in my heart that eventually Liam and I would get married, but I didn't know when. I kept my concerns to myself, but I was worried about moving the kids into a new school in two years or so, which is when he thought he would want to take the next big step and get married. By then, Michael would be a junior, Angelica would be going into sophomore year, and I knew that would not be a good time to make the switch.

One day, while working in the guidance office, I nonchalantly had a conversation with a woman named Dale, who was helping in the office that day. I told her of my concerns about the kids, their grades, and the fact that I really didn't know when Liam would want to get married. Let's face it, he was forty-four, had never married before, and was content with his life and setup. I knew he loved me, but marriage was going to be a huge leap for him.

Dale looked at me and said something I had never thought of and maybe never would have. "Why don't you and the kids move to New Jersey now, like this summer, and they can start school in the fall? You don't have to get married."

She went on to say that I was living alone anyway in the condo, so why not rent an apartment or look for a condo in New Jersey. The kids could start school sooner rather than later, and Liam and I would be in closer proximity and could spend more time together. The forty-five-minute ride was getting old anyway.

I pondered these thoughts for quite some time. I never discussed with anyone else. I was just letting the idea marinate to see if I thought it could work.

Then one Sunday a couple of months later, I was getting ready to leave Liam's house after another lovely weekend with him in New Jersey. I would be meeting my ex-husband at the usual Dunkin' Donuts to exchange the kids and get back to our lives in. Right before I was ready to say good-bye, I blurted out the idea about moving to New Jersey and the plan I had come up with in the office with Dale.

We sat across from each other in his living room. I spoke very matter-of-factly and calmly. He listened and then very calmly and sweetly said to me, "Well, if you are going to move here and uproot the kids, I think we should get married."

What? Wait! Was that a proposal?

I started insisting that getting married was not what I was talking about and that it was not necessary to get married right then. I did not want to force anything; I just wanted to move down to New

Jersey and let the kids start school, and I would find a job. He insisted that he wanted the kids to know that if they were going to move to another state and leave everything they knew, they should also know that he was committed to them and to their mom. (Can you see why I love this man so much?)

My head was spinning as I drove home. I had a huge smile on my face and kept thinking, *Was that a proposal? Is this really happening?* I think we were both a little in shock. We talked a little later that night. Both of us were kind of like, "Okay, let's do this." Liam would later joke that I tricked him into it that day.

It never occurred to me that marriage would be his response, but it made me really happy. My heart was full of love, anticipation, and excitement for my life with Liam. It was everything I had hoped for and more—in many good ways and in many challenging ways. I was thrilled to be marrying him, and once it actually sunk in, we started to tell everyone and make plans. Everyone was thrilled, and I think his long-time friends and family were in shock. They thought he would be a bachelor forever.

I don't know why, but I never thought I would get a ring or "get engaged." I wasn't expecting that to happen for some reason; it was not even on my radar. So on a typical Wednesday night, when Liam was coming over for dinner, you can image my surprise when he pulled out a ring just as I was serving my chicken stir-fry.

To this day, I'm not exactly sure what he said, because I was blindsided and in shock because of the beautiful ring he was presenting to me. It was a single round diamond on a plain platinum setting—simply elegant, beautiful, and sparkly. I screamed, cried, hugged him, and jumped around the kitchen a few times. All thoughts of dinner went out of my head as I started phoning my tribe one by one —and one by one they started showing up at the condo on Marks Place. It was an exciting night filled with love and hope.

The night we were engaged was May 2002, and the rest of the year was a whirlwind of change and movement. We went to an architect and came up with plans to knock most of Liam's existing house down and build our new home around that. I guess I'm not good at reading architectural plans because I didn't realize how big the house would be or how much of the old one would come down until I arrived on the property one day and saw a small blue tarp that looked like a teepee. The house was gone.

We were also planning our wedding, which would take place on October at the same lodge we had stayed for the Good Will Games in Lake Placid. Liam and I drove up to Lake Placid that spring and stayed at same hotel where we had fallen in love three years earlier. We were so excited and so happy. We stopped in at our favorite pub across the street for lunch, which was customary before checking in. Then we headed over to the lodge. It was on the shore of Lake Placid and was beautiful and majestic. It burned down just a few years later and was rebuilt into an even grander hotel.

Liam and I walked around the grounds before meeting the event planner. We planned an intimate wedding with just ten people, including us. We decided that we would say our vows outside on the terrace overlooking the lake (weather permitting) or in front of one of their beautiful fireplaces on the lower level. Our reception and cocktails would be in the elegant wine cellar. I loved that room, with its exposed stone and Adirondack chandeliers. It had a massive, wooden gothic table and was filled by bottles of wine and champagne—simply magnificent and romantic. We would order from the restaurant menu, since we were a small group. It was the easiest party I ever planned.

Liam and I practically skipped back to our hotel and popped a bottle of champagne off the balcony of our room. We sat down on the balcony and once again were amazed that we had found each other. We toasted to our love and our future.

Chapter 15

New Beginnings, New Jersey

We said our good-byes to Marks place in late August and moved into a rental home in New Jersey. It was an older, charming house on a corner lot. We called it Gretchen's House because the owner's name was Gretchen and she was a tyrant about her home. There were notes everywhere about how to close this gently or not to use this drawer. It was fully furnished and stocked and very comfortable.

Sticking with our plan of modeling good morals for the children, Liam took the large master bedroom. Michael had the middle room with the scary closet that led to the attic, and Angelica and I took the very adorable back bedroom with dormers and slanted walls.

It was a busy time from moving into the rental house to getting the kids situated in their new schools to building the house to planning two weddings. We had decided to have a second reception in November on Thanksgiving weekend for our friends and family that were not with us in October and it was a bigger deal, so it required more planning. So to say I was busy is an understatement, but it was all, good, amazing, and exciting.

The kids started at their new school in September while I was overseeing the house building with Liam We had to pick out everything for an entire house—from kitchen cabinets to light switches. It was exciting and exhausting. By the time it came to choose what color to stain the wood floors, I could not think straight. Luckily, Liam is a perfectionist and paid attention to every finite detail. When my brain felt like mush, he would slow down and figure out what to do next. Our home is a reflection of his hard work and our love. He would tell you it is a reflection of me, and it is in some ways. But he really put his heart and soul into our home, and you can see it in every detail.

The big day came in October, and we took off for the Adirondack's on a stunning, crisp fall morning. We drove up with a small caravan, consisting of Liam's brother, wife and their two daughters and our friends Sue and Joe. Michael and Angelica were in the back seat and we were all filled with anticipation. It was a gorgeous fall day, and the foliage was bursting out in the loveliest colors. We arrived by noontime and had lunch at our favorite pub before settling into our rooms. We had the Birds Eye View Suite again which was where we'd stayed three years earlier during the Goodwill Games. It was very nostalgic. When we checked into our room, the fireplace was ablaze, and the room was filled with flowers and champagne from friends and family.

We rested a bit before meeting everyone for dinner at a restaurant that we loved in the cozy, artsy down town area. We later came back to the lodge and sat by one of the outdoor fireplaces. Liam had bought a very special edition of Grand Mariner for me, so we found some glasses at the bar and filled our snifters while sitting around the fire and talking about our excitement for the wedding the next day. The Grand Marnier was smooth and sweet, and the fire was so warming I felt encapsulated with warmth and love. I could not remember being happier.

Waking up the next morning felt like a dream. It was finally happening. We were getting married, and Michael and Angelica were our maid of honor and best man. On paper, they actually were not because of their ages. We had to have Liam's brother, Dan and my friend Sue, sign the marriage license.

We got ourselves ready for the day and took off to the dining room for breakfast. Breakfast at the lodge was always a treat: homemade granola, yogurt, fruit, fresh-squeezed juice, and any other breakfast item you could think of. It was a rainy day, but nothing could dampen my joy. I could have cared less about the weather. It could have poured for all I cared. Anyway, I understood it's good luck when it rains on your wedding day.

After breakfast, Angelica; my sister-in-law Linda and her daughters, Samantha and Kim; and I all went to the salon to get our hair done. I chose an updo, and when we got back to the room, I did my own makeup. I got ready in Sue's room, which was actually the Honeymoon Suite, so that Liam would not see me until we were ready to say our vows. Sue poured me a glass of champagne and fed me chocolate as I applied my makeup. It had been pouring rain since we woke up, but nothing could possibly dampen my mood. The weather had no bearing on the joy in my heart and soul that day.

Angelica was getting ready with us, and my son Michael —being Michael —could not understand why I was in seclusion and why he could not see me. He came upstairs to the room and insisted he be let in to see his mom. He can be very stubborn that way.

The photographer arrived, and we took some pictures in the room; then it was time to join Liam and the rest of the group. Walking down the stairs in my gown with my children beside me felt surreal. I was so excited and could not wait to see my groom. I entered the room, and there he was, looking so handsome in his suit in front of the fireplace.

He took my hand, and we stood together before the justice of the peace. We had written our own vows, and I cried throughout saying mine. Liam's words were beyond profound and beautiful.

Our wedding vows on October, 2002:

Liam to Tia:

> As I stand here preparing to make this wonderful commitment of marriage with the woman I love, I look out to these majestic, awe-inspiring mountains, and I realize that they are symbols of our relationship, commitment, and love for each other. For those mountains were not created overnight. Like our deep love and commitment, they will endure until the end of time. You know, before I had you, Michael and Angelica in my life, if you asked me what a tear was, I would have told you it was mere water and salt. Today, however, if you ask the same question of me, I can tell you about the love of a man and a woman and the joys and challenges of raising a beautiful family. I will

be forever be humbled by the gift of love the three of you have given me.

I love you.

Tia to Liam:

> I consider it an honor to be the one you have chosen as your life's partner. You are a brave man to marry a woman with two children; it is not and easy task—yet you manage it with courage and grace. I cannot imagine a better role model for my children. I know God has brought us all together, and we are truly blessed. Today, our wedding day is only a brief day in time, and although our vows are spoken in a matter of minutes, they are promises that will last a lifetime. When we leave this ceremony, today I will be a better person because of you. Because of your love and trust, my life is fulfilled and has a new beginning. I promise to be a true, faithful, and loving wife. I promise to respect you and to be honest with you always. I promise to share with you all that is to come. To give and receive, to speak and to listen. May my heart be your shelter and my arms your home always.

I love you.

Right after we completed our vows, the rain stopped, and the sun came out. We were able to go outside and get some stunning pictures with the fall foliage afterward. Our small group then headed back inside for our cocktail party. Champagne flowed, and Michael and Dan gave heart-warming speeches. Before long, we were gathered in the magnificent wine cellar, looking at menus and awaiting our feast. It was a beautiful night—complete with a full moon.

We ate, laughed, drank wine, and pinched ourselves some more. It could not have been a dreamier, more ethereal day. My children were with me, I was married to the man I loved, and the future was brighter than ever before. I felt safe, loved, and most of all, blessed.

The next day, after another hearty Adirondack breakfast, we loaded up the cars and headed back to reality and our new lives together. There was still much to do with planning our reception for our extended family and friends and with building our dream home.

We celebrated Thanksgiving at the rental house, and our reception that weekend was just as amazing as our wedding day, though not as intimate. We had about sixty-five of our closest friends and family with us. The band played all night, and we danced, dined on the most delicious food, and celebrated life and love.

Chapter 16

Forgiveness: The Most Important F Word

Forgiveness is not always easy. At times, it feels more painful than the wound we suffered, to forgive the one that inflicted it. Yet, there is no peace without forgiveness.

—Marianne Williamson

I have spent the last twenty-five years and probably most of my life being angry with my mom. When she was alive, I was so codependent with her that my anger was manifested as self-loathing. If she was having a good day (and there were not many), I was having a good day.

I call, and she is sober. *Good day.*

I see her, and she is not too tripped on pills. *Good day.*

I call her, and she actually sounds happy, and she's sober. *Great day.*

I see her, and she's lucid. *Great day.*

All the other days, I caused myself to suffer.

I did not know any better. She was my mom. I loved her. I needed her, and I wanted her to be well. But what I wanted more than anything else was for her to be my mother, to act like a mother, to love me the way a mother loves her daughter.

To say it was easy would be an understatement. She was my drug in a way. I was so worried that she would get hurt or die. I was so worried, but I had to let go. I had to be a mom to my son and a wife to my husband and a friend to myself. I had to stop being the mother to my mother. Too many days and nights had been wasted. I could never be present in my life if I continued on that path. I needed a life.

I felt relief when she died because I was at that point well along on my journey of healing. I knew she was in a better place without pain and suffering.

I recognized her as a lost soul, a shell of a person she once was, and it was her time.

I don't think I had ever forgiven my mother for all the years of craziness: Coming home from school and finding her passed out drunk. Embarrassed to have friends over. Her violently angry outbursts. The seizures. Her constant drama, her arrests, her shoplifting, her coming home covered in blood because she fell. Strangers taking her home. Calls from strangers who had found her. She never came to a school function or even my graduation. She got drunk at my wedding. The list goes on and on.

But the time has come to practice the greatest F word of all: *forgiveness*.

I was always able to forgive my dad for anything and everything and to say that he did the best with what he knew. I think it's because I always felt loved, protected, and taken care of by him.

I knew my mother loved me, but she could not show me. She was not capable.

But it's time to forgive on my journey and in my fifty-fifth year of life. It's time.

So Mom, I forgive you.

I have let go of the hurt and the pain. I release the shame and embarrassment, and I see you through the eyes of love. I know that you were suffering and in pain and unable to heal your own wounds. I know you were fighting a battle so great we will never understand.

I thank you for what you did do for me to the best of your ability. I thank you for the lessons. I would not be who I am today if you were not a part of my journey. I pray for you today, knowing you are in the hands of God and the angels, in a place much more beautiful than here.

You are at peace. I love you, Mom. I love you with every ounce of my six-year-old soul and my heart today.

Love, Me

Chapter 17

Home at Last: Somewhere in New Jersey

The following May, the house was completed, and we all moved in and settled down. I felt like I was truly home for the first time. I felt very at peace with my new home and my new life this quaint town in New Jersey. The kids made friends and were happy to be settled. The neighborhood is small and safe. The entire town is a mile wide, and the kids get to walk wherever they need to go: school, friends' houses, or down to the 7-Eleven for giant Slurpees.

Once the boxes were cleared, I had the house somewhat decorated. That isn't my strong point, but I managed with some help. It's not the most important thing to me. I'd rather have my mind and soul pulled together than be worried about hanging artwork or curtains. So I started to think about what I wanted to be when I grew up.

This was the first time in my life that I had the time and space to focus on myself. I was forty years old, and I wanted to accomplish so much. My kids were practically grown, and I knew it would a matter of a few years before they would spread their wings and leave the nest. They are and always will be my greatest accomplishments, but it was time for me to soar, too.

I finally got to cook my first Feast of the Seven Fishes our first Christmas in our new home. Now, I have changed it up a bit by making most of the fish into a delicious *zuppe di pesce* (fish soup). I still always start with a cold seafood salad, and it has been a hit with my husband's big Irish and Estonian family. At least one night out of the year, everyone is Italian.

I knew then that whatever I decided to do with my career, it had be something in the health, wellness, or healing field. I eventually set my sights on a nutrition school that was mind, body, and spirit oriented. I loved the idea. Around the same time, I picked up my yoga practice again at a local studio, continued journaling, dabbled with meditation again, and found a new therapist to keep me in check. There are always so many layers to uncover, and I wanted to keep growing and to keep healing my wounded heart.

The best decision I ever made was going to nutrition school. I was always into natural remedies, healing, and health. I realized it was my true passion, and I finally had the time and the money to invest in my calling. I attended the Institute of Integrative Nutrition (IIN). My education equipped me with much insight into nutrition and preventive care, with a focus on holistic nutrition and practical lifestyle techniques. With my love of health and wellness and a strong desire to help others, I embarked on my journey.

I loved every minute of going to school and learning about nutrition, health, wellness, and how to feed my body and soul. With my passion for food, health, and wellness, I was in my happy place every weekend at IIN. I loved the drive into the city every Saturday and Sunday morning. The roads were empty and quiet as I zipped over the George Washington Bridge and made my way to the Time Warner Building at Columbus Circle. I could not wait to get to class to absorb all that would be taught to me. The teachers and speakers that took the stage each weekend were some of my gurus and heroes.

My first spiritual teacher was Debbie Ford. When I'd read her book twenty-five years before, *The Dark Side of the Light Chasers*, my heart nearly exploded. I started to embrace all that I was—my darkness and my light. There she was one Saturday morning, all those years later, on stage in front of me, still talking about embracing our weaknesses and our dark side so that we could have the freedom to live authentically. On that day, I finally started to understand what Debbie was talking about.

My work within myself today is still to recognize, embrace, and ultimately love all aspects of my shadow, my light, and dark sides. Yes, it's work, but the rewards have been illuminating. I don't know where I would be today without my inner journey and spiritual practice.

Before graduation, I started my health coaching business, and started seeing clients. I love the work of guiding people to higher levels of health and happiness. You know you are in the right place, doing the work you're meant for, when your job doesn't feel like work.

I've been a health and lifestyle coach for more than seven years now. Although I do work with men, my passion is coaching women, either one-on-one or through women's wellness group coaching workshops. My mission is to empower, enlighten, and love as many women as I can, so they can live their best lives. They say you teach what you need to learn. I know that as I teach and help people heal, I also am healing.

Michael and Angelica have grown into two of the most amazing human beings a mother could pray for. They are smart, kind, and loving with big, generous hearts. They are my two hearts that beat outside my body, and I am blessed to be their mom. They've moved into their own homes now, so Liam and I have a big, beautiful empty nest.

We love our home, and anyone who walks through the doors says they feel the love and peace. I have never been happier in my life than I am here and now in this sweet little town in New Jersey.

On October, 2012, Liam and I renewed our vows:

Liam to Tia

> As I stand here on our tenth wedding anniversary, at the age of fifty-five, I have to thank you, Tia, for in just ten short years, you have given me a lifetime of happiness. I know the next fifty-five years will be filled with untold joys.
>
> you have shown me the true definition of success. Through your love, you have made me a successful man. All my adult life, logic and numbers have been my barometer of happiness. That is not

enough. You have taught me to embrace my feelings along with your endless love. Love does not need a reason to be; it just is.

After a decade of forming our family with our children, I realize that just the world of logic does not lead to happiness, and with that, I have come to the most important discovery of my life. Had God not guided us together, I would have never found the mysterious equations of love and acceptance.

I am only here today because of you. You are the reason I am. You are all my reasons. I will love you to the end of time.

Tia to Liam

I could not have imagined when Kara told me about you so many years ago the journey you and I would embark on. She spoke to me of a wonderful guy who was handsome and sweet and had beautiful blue eyes, and she could not wait for us to meet. We had our first date, and the rest is history.

I am so amazingly blessed to have you arrive into my life and into the lives of my children.

I could not have asked for a better role model—a man with a beautiful heart of gold, generous beyond measure, insightful, and so kind.

Thank you for loving me the way I never knew and only dreamt was possible.

You remain and always will be my love, my rock, my shelter from the storm, and my safe spot to land. I love you.

Liam and I continue forward in our life. There have been struggles blending a family and all that comes with it, but the love and good times outweigh the struggles. We grow more in love every year. This year we will celebrate fifteen years of marriage, and I could not have wished for a better man to spend my life with. I still pinch myself sometimes when I look into his eyes and see the love he has for me. He continues to be my love, my rock and my constant shelter from the storm.

Journal Page

Journal Page

Journal Page

Journal Page

Journal Page

Journal Page

Journal Page

Journal Page

Journal Page

Journal Page